Books by Robert Bagg

Madonna of the Cello: Poems

The Scrawny Sonnets and Other Narratives

Euripides, *Hippolytos* (translation with introduction and notes)

Euripides, *The Bakkhai* (translation with introduction and notes)

THE BAKKHAI

THE BAKKHAI

BY EURIPIDES

Translated by ROBERT BAGG

University of Massachusetts Press   Amherst

Frontispiece courtesy of Staatliche
Antikensammlungen und Glyptothek München

Library of Congress Catalog Card Number 77-90732
ISBN 0-87023-190-1 (cloth); 0-87023-191-x (paper)
Library of Congress Cataloging in Publication Data
appear on the last printed page of the book.
Designed by Mary Mendell

for Thomas Gould

Contents

Every classical Greek play has a strangeness at its heart, something alien or disorienting to its modern audience. Often the strangeness derives from a Greek cultural phenomenon for which we have no exact counterpart: for example, the passionate chastity of Hippolytos, or the Furies in the *Oresteia* who hound only murderers of blood-kin. In *The Bakkhai* there is a strangeness not only in the ecstatic and bloody cult of Dionysos, but in the horrifying emphasis placed on Pentheus' sudden assumption of a maenad's female costume and sensibility. Because a play's deepest meanings are likely to be inextricable from this kind of cultural strangeness, we must attend to it. We need to know such things as why the Dionysian experience exerted such a powerful appeal, and how masculine and feminine sexual natures were perceived by the Greeks, if we wish to understand the extraordinary use the play makes of these cultural facts.

The prevalence of antique concerns—such as ritual pollution and purification—which cause a contemporary reader difficulty, has in recent times led scholars, especially the English, to argue that Greek drama is more parochial and time-bound than once thought, preoccupied with issues more alive to fifth-century Athenians than to us. Since the Renaissance, the humanist tradition has honored Greek tragedy as an inexhaustible oracle speaking to the permanent human condition; but some modern scholars ask whether even the most famous plays really address the same large universal issues that we find troubling and fascinating. It has been argued that, for instance, the excruciating truths *Oedipus the King* presents concerning parents and children should be translated into a drama about inherited curses and the pollution arising from kin murder. *The Bakkhai,* however, has largely escaped such dilution. Its profundity and psychological sophistication continue to be admired by nearly all who study it in Greek or in translation. Some of the finest modern criticism has illuminated the absorbing complexity and savage freshness of this play. Frederich Nietzsche, W. K. C. Guthrie, E. R. Dodds, and especially R. P. Winnington-Ingram (whose *Euripides and Dionysos* is the most rewarding book in English about a single Greek play), have shown that the forces Dionysos wields are real, forces that no man in any age can afford to ignore: a source of supreme joy and a danger as destructive as any in life.[1]

The Bakkhai is a play about the advent of that knowledge, but

---

[1] Euripides, *The Bacchae,* ed. E. R. Dodds (Oxford University Press, 1963); W. K. C. Guthrie, *The Greeks and Their Gods* (Boston: The Beacon Press, 1955), pp. 145–82; Frederich Nietzsche, *The Birth of Tragedy* (New York: Gordon, 1974); R. P. Winnington-Ingram, *Euripides and Dionysos* (Amsterdam: Adolf M. Hakkert, 1969).

it is also about resistance to it and the fate of those who resist. Some of Dionysos' ancient cult names suggest only his healthy and life-nurturing role: he is the Power in the Tree, the Blossombringer and Fruitbringer, the Abundance of Life. Plutarch speaks of him as the god of all natural liquids. In E. R. Dodds' words, he is "not only the liquid fire in the grape, but the sap thrusting in a young tree, the blood pounding in the veins of a young animal, all the mysterious and uncontrollable tides that ebb and flow in the life of nature." [2] Inherent in the sweet energy of all these liquids, however, are potential cruelty and death. We know that the reward promised to those who worshipped Dionysos was a purifying religious experience which brought the god's essence and power surging into his devotee, and that wearing Dionysos' masks and animal skins, acting in his plays, drinking his wine and dancing his mountain rituals were all ways to put the god inside the worshipper. But the most powerful and climactic acts seem to have been the sacraments of *sparagmos* and *omophagia.* The first is the tearing apart of a live animal victim; the second is the eating of an animal's raw and warm flesh, thus ingesting the god, who is reborn inside one. In that act, which is always described in the ancient texts as one of joy, the animal was felt to be Dionysos himself, from whom his worshippers took sudden godlike ecstasy and strength.

This transformation of initiates into Bakkhai is the central event in Dionysian religion, a fact that the title of the play may well mark. We can get into trouble, to be sure, if we expect a play's traditional name to enlighten us about its author's intentions. We cannot assume that the name by which we know a play was chosen by its author, for in some instances a play's name was not settled until a generation after its first production. (Generally, when the story of a major character coincided with a play's plot, that play became known by the character's name, as did the *Agamemnon* and the *Antigone*. A play lacking an obvious central figure was usually named after its Chorus.) It is fairly easy to understand why this play did not become known as the *Pentheus* or the *Dionysos*. Though Pentheus does suffer because a god hates him, and though his destruction forms the basic plot, he is never presented as a stirring or morally powerful figure; rather, he appears as a strident but inept advocate of his own cause. On the other hand, Dionysos' effortless domination of Pentheus offers none of the struggle, suffering and moral enlightenment that the hero of a tragedy was expected to exhibit. Therefore *The Bakkhai* was named (whether by intent or default) after its Chorus, the women who followed Dionysos from Asia to Greece. They are indeed at the center of the action, not in the sense

[2] Dodds, p. xii.

that their story is the plot itself, but because the divine force they advocate is the true subject of the tragedy.

When this divine force, embodied in the god Dionysos, appears in Greek legend, it is almost invariably met with resistance. Typical is the story Homer tells of Lycurgus the Thracian who hunted Dionysos and his nurses on the sacred mountain, Nysa, drove them into the sea, and was in turn blinded for his crime (*Iliad,* 6.130 ff.). In later versions Lycurgus was variously torn apart by horses or panthers, walled into a cave, or forced to cut off his own legs. In the accounts which describe the spread of his cult, Dionysos rarely triumphs without bitter opposition from some leader or faction of the people he seeks to convert. The myths are so consistent on this point that we must wonder whether an actual historical memory underlies plays like *The Bakkhai.*

It would not be true to say that Dionysos was a god who appeared on the scene at a substantially later date than his fellow Olympians, and was thereby resented and fought as an interloper. His name appears in Homer, as we have seen; it also has been found on Mycenaean tablets. Dionysos, the god, goes back as far in time as our records do. Yet his antiquity does not prove that his religion could not have swept Greece at a much later period, in waves of much-resisted hysteria, in the same way Christian evangelism has swept the world in waves centuries after its inception. It is possible, therefore, that behind the story of the play—the coming of Dionysos to Thebes, the young king's active resistance to him, and revenge exacted by the god—lies an actual memory of such an incident in the Theban past. If nothing but such a memory "explained" the play, however, it would interest only antiquarians. The continued power of the play leads us to ask why a god would be regularly and stubbornly celebrated as a bringer of joy, a joy strenuously opposed by established authority. I would agree with those who conclude that the practices that the Greeks associated with Dionysos provoked and fed those appetites for release and joy that all established and orderly societies in any era must continually suppress—since they can neither be reconciled to ordinary ambitions nor killed outright. Such a conclusion explains both the peculiar form the Dionysos stories take—always one of resistance, triumph and punishment— and the intense interest these stories arouse long after the cults themselves have vanished.

The Greek word for those who banded together in Dionysian cults was *thiasos,* a word which is possibly pre-Greek in origin. We do not know what its earliest context was, but it came to refer to all kinds of sympathetic social bondings, from literary discussion groups to the kind of hysteria that turns crowds into raging superbeings. (Some modern examples of the *thiasos* come readily to mind: from bland ties of social life to the emotionalism of war, sport and ecstatic religion—all the institutional or customary means by which we try to enlarge ourselves, seeking to be stronger, freer, happier, by adding others to ourselves and, by taking as our own the personality of the group, rise above our ordinary selves.)

The Dionysian *thiasos* ranges from the calm reasoning loyalty to the god found in the Chorus of Bakkhai all the way to that other band of possessed women roaming the hills and tearing animals limb from limb. What they have in common is a shedding (temporarily at least) of the limitations of individual responsibility. In almost all cases the members of the *thiasos* yield the job of testing reality and making moral distinctions to an adored leader; in *The Bakkhai* this leader is the god Dionysos. It is even possible that in all *thiasoi,* the worshipper experienced the leader as the god himself.

What the civil authorities feared in the pure form of the Dionysian *thiasos* was its unconcern with anything but its own gratification; its seduction of women from their homes; its violent potential; its immunity to responsible leadership. Historically, what seems to have happened in Greece is that city-states found ways of taming the Dionysiac. In Athens, a little more than a century before the first production of *The Bakkhai* c. 405 B.C., the tyrant Pisistratus had brought a version of popular rural Dionysian celebrations into the city and granted them an official glory second only to those of Athena herself. A generation later when the democracy became established, leaders of the people were quite willing to retain this official recognition of Dionysos. As the Chorus says repeatedly, he is the god of ordinary, unpretentious men and women. His appeal to the humble explains a feature of the play that might puzzle a modern reader: the insistence by the Chorus that whoever accepts Dionysos accepts common wisdom and balanced good sense. This seems a startlingly tame requirement from the god of ecstatic joy. We do know that these virtues of restraint were popular with the average Athenian. But the skill with which Euripides overwhelms these words, *sophia* (wisdom) and *sophrosyne* (balanced good sense) by the brutal shock of their contexts in the play, shows how these words have become perverted from their traditional significance.

As Dionysos, Kadmos, Tiresias and the Messenger use it, "wisdom" becomes a synonym for mindless and tenacious conformity, for avoidance of risk, quite the reverse of the adventurous and sharply drawn definitions this word acquired in the circle of Socrates and Plato. "Wisdom," as the Chorus uses it in the fourth choral ode, means exultation in naked power:

What is wisdom?
                    When the gods
crush our enemies, their heads cowed
under the hard fist of our power,
that is glory!

The weight given such words as *sophia* in *The Bakkhai* is not merely paradoxical, it is an instance of a point Euripides makes in various ways throughout the play. The Dionysian experience appears to exalt equally both the wisdom and the murder. But Euripides will show us that the accommodation is finally an illusion: only the murder is real. Whatever seems a positive virtue, whether it be wisdom, moderation or piety, when infected by the Dionysian spirit, is soon dominated by its opposite: folly, excess, blasphemy.

The fact that life at its sweetest and happiest and most carefree is vulnerable to fury and pain is shown frequently in the play. It seems a lesson Euripides' god most wishes to teach, for as Dionysos says of himself, he is "the extremest of gods — pure terror / to humankind, and yet pure loving kindness." The impression the play gives of the new life offered by Dionysos to his initiates is nevertheless at first undeniably rich in pleasure and excitement. The Chorus speaks of the Dionysiac as a kind of happiness, or *eudaimonia,* which means literally "having a permanent life-enhancing relation to a divinity." He who worships Dionysos, however, will not find permanent safety and joy, for the god's strength is only in him while he is acting unconsciously; it is absent when he is conscious.

The Theban maenads in the play are happy on the mountain at first because of what they leave behind (here I adapt Winnington-Ingram's felicitous summary of the positive and negative aspects of Dionysian happiness): the duties, drudgery, boredom of civilized life; the limitations of individuality; the burden of self-knowledge; the painful effort of thought; concern for past and future. Such cares vanish when the initiate's personality dissolves into that of her sisters in the *thiasos.* Those are all the things one escapes. What the maenads discover in Dionysos, we learn from the Herdsman's account, is an immediate, unthinking joy in the present, delight in a whole new life of vivid simple action: feasting, purifying rites, hymn-singing, making ivy-crowns and wands, magical outpourings of milk, wine and honey, suckling of young animals, wild ecstatic mountain dancing, hunting and tearing to pieces wild creatures, eating their flesh, and finally, deep exhausted sleep.[3] Here are two accounts of this life, the first by the Herdsman, the second by the Chorus:

[3] Winnington-Ingram, pp. 156–57.

> Then one struck her wand
> to a rock—out jumps icy springwater!
> Another pushed hers gently into the pasture
> feeling for Bakkhos—she found the god
> who made wine flood up right there!
> Women eager for milk raked the meadow
> with their fingers until it oozed out
> fresh and white.
> Raw honey was dripping
> in sweet threads from their wands.
>
> The mountain goes sweet with Bakkhos!
> He's there in the maenad,
> his fawnskin's on her body—
> out of the running pack
> she drops to the earth!
> She kills in blood, she devours in joy
> the raw flesh of a goat, and is hurled
> back to the mountains
> of Phrygia and Lydia,
> cried on by the Loud God, whose cry
> runs through her.

Euripides here and throughout satisfies our curiosity to know what maenads experienced. His skill is such that we see also what they lose—the power to connect and weigh, forethought and after-thought, knowledge of where they are and what they are doing. The maenads find equal happiness in suckling wolf cubs and rending heifers apart. Wine, music, love-making and wild dance are the substance of Dionysian religion—scenes which appear by the hundred on Greek drinking pots dedicated to the god—and each of these may become a doorway to oblivion. In the mutual stimulus of the group, emotion is more easily shared than is thought, emotion which grants the maenad a deep if illusory peace of mind. The connection between animal joy and human savagery is reinforced by each successive choral ode, and is perfected in Agave's great final scene when she must recognize, step by reasoning step, that the head of the beast she killed exultantly in a flash of fury is that of her son, Pentheus.

The most convincing and exciting way to portray Dionysos' power would be to show us his maenads completely under the god's control, performing *sparagmos* and *omophagia,* handling snakes, tapping wine from the earth. But this was dramaturgically impossible and aesthetically risky. Failing that, we are given a dramatic correlative—controlled musical dances of the Chorus, vivid description of wilder events offstage, and a realistic and thrilling psychic

(margin note: → internalized Dionysiac)

battle between man and god. It would be more accurate to describe
this last dramatization of the Dionysiac as a confrontation between
the god himself and the internalized Dionysiac within his mortal
opponent.

This power of Dionysos as it appears onstage is not at all a
delicious intoxication; it is an uncanny verbal mastery and psychological astuteness wielded by a young god, both calm and charisma-
tic, who in the course of a few scenes destroys an equally young
man. The god who destroys Pentheus' mind by reducing it to a
single, mad craving is able to do so because, as Dodds and Winnington-Ingram have argued, Dionysos has an ally in the enemy camp:
"May not the lust for power and praise which Pentheus has, be
equally the source of a Dionysiac frenzy? . . . If Pentheus is obsessed
with curiosity and desire, the victory of Dionysos is half won already." [4]

The manic and obsessive nature of Pentheus stands out sharply
against the smooth, evasive Dionysos whom Euripides has created.
The pair first meet when Pentheus, reacting to news that all the
Theban women have been lured into secret and probably lewd
mountain revels by an attractive long-haired Bakkhic priest from
Lydia, orders this stranger captured and brought before him. After
sizing up his prisoner in words that reveal fascination with his physical beauty, Pentheus attempts to extract information about the rites:
"Tell me about these mysteries of yours. . . . What does this ritual
do—I mean for those who join it?" In reply, the Stranger tantalizes,
frustrates, insults. The direction taken by Pentheus' eager probing
in search of a shocking reality behind the rituals reveals that his
interest is not only that of a righteous magistrate punishing a
troublemaker, but also that of someone excluded from events which
painfully attract him.

Throughout the play Pentheus will continue to be deflected
from his kingly office into the whirlpool of his own obsessions: "You
tell me nothing with so much cunning/ it makes me ache to hear
more" is one of his early admissions to Dionysos. Where are the
answers the Stranger withholds? Somewhere on Cithaeron, Pentheus
thinks, in the dance, the ritual, in the furtive sex acts he imagines
the maenads enjoying. But the calm skill of the Stranger has shifted
our attention to the inner life of Pentheus. We begin to see Dionysos
as a malevolent psychoanalyst working to unearth some destructive
urge, some appalling fact which motivates Pentheus but of which
he is ignorant. The god uses verbal wit as his mode of exposure:
dozens of double-pronged sallies that say one thing to Pentheus'
suspicious political brain, and another to his seething unconscious

(margin note: Dionysos as psychoanalyst)

[4] Winnington-Ingram, pp. 54 and 46; compare Dodds, p. 172.

and to us. Dionysos several times taunts Pentheus for his incomprehension: "True wisdom stupefies a fool." When Dionysos says the rites happen at night because "night helps us to feel holy," Pentheus' own prurience surfaces in his reply: "You mean night helps you to rape women."

The more Dionysos succeeds in exacerbating Pentheus' erotic fantasies, the more anger Pentheus conceives for the agile Lydian Stranger. After seizing his Bakkhic wand and cutting off his long hair, Pentheus tries to chain the god in a stable; when Dionysos escapes with frightening ease Pentheus switches his fury to the next available target, the maenads on Cithaeron who he learns from the Herdsman are performing miracles of pleasure and savagery, all of which Pentheus feels as a personal humiliation.

Rage and attempted or threatened violence are his instinctive response to any threat to his power. A painted or sculpted mask of outrage must have been worn by the actor who played Pentheus in the Greek theater. The Chorus in particular traces Pentheus' brutality back to his kin, the *Spartoi* or "Sown Men," who grew from the teeth of a giant snake. Kadmos had killed the snake and on Athena's advice sowed the Theban earth with its teeth. The seeds grew into savage warriors fully armed who immediately began killing each other until only five were left; from these five, which included Pentheus' father, Echion, whose name means "the Snake," all the noble families of Thebes were descended. The many references to Pentheus as son of a Sown Man are never complimentary, but hurled at him in hostility. Even when Pentheus invokes his own ancestry he reminds the audience of a superhuman reptilian element in his hostility to Dionysos. The god in his prologue and Agave in her moments of deluded triumph both speak of Pentheus as a "godfighter." The implication is that Pentheus is an enemy of the gods by birth and inheritance.

Actually, within Pentheus, then, are two warring kinds of divinity—the Titanic race of Mother Earth, enemies of Dionysos; and the Dionysiac itself. (According to an Orphic myth mankind itself is just such a mixture: the Titans who devoured Dionysos after his first birth were themselves destroyed by the thunderbolt of Zeus, but when their scattered flesh touched Earth mankind sprang into being.) The struggle within Pentheus dramatized in our play may therefore be seen as a reawakening of the ancient struggle between the two kinds of divinity, with the Dionysiac winning as usual. The victory, however, is not one of civilization and order.

When it comes—this victory of the Dionysos within Pentheus —it comes with the ease and swiftness of events in a dream. When Dionysos asks suddenly, "Would you like to see maenads/ sitting together, up there on the mountain?" Pentheus' instant acceptance and later acquiescence to maenad costume declare a true desire, one long held in check by his fear of disruptive innovation, his dread of humiliation, his contempt for women and any unmanly act. Pentheus' furious scorn of Bakkhic things as effeminate betrays the obsessions which the god will exploit: extravagant rage had here masked, as often in mankind generally, insatiable fascination.

The futility of a godfighter's mission is this: all the energies of resistance must contribute to the ultimate triumph of the god. The knife-edge on which are balanced Pentheus' impulse to fury and his longing to surrender, is suggested by these words, spoken as he tries to "decide" whether to put on a maenad's costume or war against them: "I'll either come out fighting/ or put myself in your hands." Putting himself in the Stranger's care is something Pentheus does explicitly in his final scene. "I want you to take care of me," he says as Dionysos straightens his hem, and later, as the pair head toward the mountain, "Show me off through the heart of Thebes."

Pentheus is as unaware of his vulnerability to Dionysos as he is of the psychic imperatives that make it possible. Dionysos accuses Pentheus of this blindness with remarkable bluntness just before Pentheus imprisons him. Says Dionysos: "Why, you're not even in command/ of your own life! You don't know/ what you are doing, or who you are." Pentheus' stunned answer to this challenge to his identity, "I am Pentheus, son of Echion and Agave," would have an echo to a Greek speaker. A Greek would hear the noun *penthos*, "grief" or "remorse," in the name Pentheus. He would hear "snake" in Echion's name. He might even hear a muted echo of the word "greatness" in Agave's name. The Greek speaker might imagine Pentheus has just said, "I am Grief, son of the Snake and the Great One." Knowledge of our birth and our parents can sometimes be the reverse of comforting. In the name his parents gave him, as in the name of his monstrous father, the audience recognizes something ominous, in spite of Pentheus' confidence that knowing one's name and family origin brings one a firm sense of identity. Soon the god will begin in earnest to disrupt Pentheus' sense of what is real.

By the time Pentheus staggers outside his palace, dazed from his hallucinatory struggles with Dionysos, Euripides has prepared us to expect Pentheus' mind to become the field of battle. In the stable Pentheus found that his tame prisoner had become a raging bull, which he sweats to rope; moments later the palace catches fire, a fire which blazes in Pentheus' mind only. A glowing image of the Stranger then appears; Pentheus slashes at it futilely with his sword. Dionysos has led Pentheus to take as real these successive hallucinations, and to try to control them with physical violence. The Stranger's smug judgment is: "He tried to fight god." Using

brute force to subdue things that force cannot control is Pentheus'
characteristic error, and the god's cool account of these futile efforts
in the palace evokes it chillingly. Pentheus will have no better luck
later trying to master the Stranger or subdue the maenads, since
the power Pentheus fears they possess derives in great part from
the awe in which he holds them. This awe is what the god distills
into those mocking, hallucinatory images which ambush Pentheus
in his own palace.

Hardly a moment will pass in the first half of the drama without Pentheus expressing rage, and it is this rage which Dionysos
defuses and transforms. Rage is a prime outlet for masculine erotic
force, but what Dionysos makes of it as he draws Pentheus under
his spell is the utter opposite of "masculinity." The transforming
process occupies the heart of the play; when we last see Pentheus
on stage he is both docile and exalted. He has just put on the
maenad's gown, wears hair like theirs, holds their green wand and
has taken the first tentative steps in their dance. He feels within
him an unlimited physical strength as he sets out to watch a scene
of maenads at revel which he hopes will satisfy an imperious craving.
To better understand this raging *eros,* now become a joyful and
sexually curious *eros,* we should recall the range of meaning *eros*
could have in Greek.

Devotees of Dionysos appear to have responded to two warring
kinds of *eros,* or "desire," one of which is lust, an egocentric and
aggressive passion. The other kind of *eros* is a yearning for peace
and well-being which is consonant with both childhood innocence
and social harmony. This contrast would be differently described
by men and by women. The Dionysian cult seems to be imagined
from the point of view of women devotees. As a consequence, the
first kind of *eros* is looked upon as absurd or ugly. In the most
common representations of the Dionysian vision—as represented on
drinking cups and other household objects—absurd lust is most
obvious in the satyr beast-men with large erect phalluses, the
would-be rapists of the always dignified Bakkhai. Because this play
is a tragedy and not a satyr play such as Euripides' *The Cyclops,*
this vision could not be enacted directly on stage, but is represented
nevertheless—in the absurd and ineffectual supermasculinity of the
young king and in the irony of his public humiliation: the revelation
that within him lies what he hates most, a feminine narcissism and
softness and yearning for oblivion.

To reveal to the world such overt feminine characteristics
would devastate any Greek male. When Pentheus says, "We are
humiliated/ when we let women act like this," he is reverting to
the Greek male's fear of women which pervades Greek literature of
the age of tragedy. We see it, for instance, in Creon's paranoiac

reaction to Antigone's rebelliousness, as well as in Jason's thoroughly justified terror of Medea. There were two aspects of this fear: fear of being dominated by women, and fear of being overwhelmed by their sexuality. Aristophanes devotes an entire play, the *Thesmaphoriazusae*, to the revenge taken by the women of Athens on Euripides for his supposed slanders against their sex.

Repeatedly during their scenes together Pentheus compliments Dionysos for understanding him so well. What Dionysos understands and exploits is that Pentheus' fear of maenads and his consequent eagerness to lead his troops against them is bound up with his obsession to visit the sexual orgies he imagines they enjoy in the hills. By suddenly arresting Pentheus' attention and posing his real wish as a tempting question, Dionysos draws Pentheus away from armed violence into a world where his desires seem miraculously susceptible to fulfillment:

DIONYSOS   . . . Would you like to see maenads
                     sitting together, up there on the mountain?
PENTHEUS   I would give all the gold I have to see that. . . .
                     Get me there quickly. Waiting is torture.
DIONYSOS   First, clothe your body in a fine linen dress.
PENTHEUS   A dress? Why are you disguising my sex?
DIONYSOS   To save your life. The maenads kill all men.

Though he fights the suggestion and must be lulled into accepting it, once Pentheus emerges from the palace in maenad garb he is delighted with his resemblance to the women in his family, and with the prospect ahead. The entire scene is supercharged with excitement. Pentheus feels in his body a clearly Dionysian physical power: he thinks he can wrench loose the entire mountain and carry it and the maenads home. Acceptance of maenad costume seems, before our eyes, to release the constraints on Pentheus: he becomes horribly joyful. Early in the play the very thought of putting on an ivy crown revolts him; now acquiescence to the god's regalia initiates him into Dionysian life. The joy released in Pentheus comes simultaneously from breaking through his fear of women and breaking through his horror of Dionysian clothes and rituals. Euripides has boldly symbolized resistance to the Dionysiac as resistance to becoming woman-like.

This representation of the Dionysiac as feminine—at once fearful and attractive—is embedded in the dramatic action of the play's final exchange between Pentheus and the god. A single, explosive word at the very climax of the exchange, as it expresses Pentheus' consuming exaltation, will express in a still more disturbing form the identity of the Dionysiac and the feminine.

In his final moments onstage Pentheus yields to a wish to

move toward infancy and be held again in his mother's arms. The ability of nostalgia to lure our adult selves back to a worry-free existence in the care of a mother could not be more powerfully shown. And since we will soon know that this same mother Agave will lead the *sparagmos,* the ritual tearing to pieces of her son, that nostalgia must seem horrible. The horror is increased by the fact that Euripides has imagined a dramatic situation in which, before our eyes, the yearning for infancy becomes an unacknowledged wish to die:

PENTHEUS   Show me off through the heart of Thebes.
            I want them all to see: I'm the man
            who will brave anything.

DIONYSOS   Indeed you will.
            The suffering of Thebes
            is on your shoulders now. Yours alone.
            Something violent lies ahead
            and you won't miss it.

                                    Come with me,
            I will see you through it.
            Someone else will bring you home.

PENTHEUS   Mother!

DIONYSOS   Yes! As a great symbol to mankind

PENTHEUS   That's my wish.

DIONYSOS   you will be carried here

PENTHEUS   What luxury!

DIONYSOS   hugged in your mother's arms.

PENTHEUS   You'll make me go
            all to pieces!

DIONYSOS   I'd have it no other way.

What Dionysos and Pentheus collaborate to imagine goes well beyond a voyeur's inspection of maenads at revel. A young man is here deliciously bemused in infantile fantasy—to be hugged and carried home from the mountains in his mother's arms. Even more extraordinary is the sentence with which Pentheus describes his fearfully astonished anticipation: *kai tryphan m' an017 anankaseis,* "You'll make me go/ all to pieces!" If translated, rather grotesquely, but so as better to suggest the amazing range of its implications, the sentence would go: "You will force me to turn loose all my luxurious feminine element!" The arresting word is the climactic one I earlier referred to, *tryphan,* a word that Dionysos immediately repeats in its nominal form, giving his sinister assent to Pentheus' unconscious prediction of what will happen to him. *Tryphan* can mean "to be licentious," "to be effeminate," or "to give oneself airs." In each of these meanings the basic gesture is one of letting go, of giving in to self-indulgence. A Greek could have heard in *tryphan* the verb *thryptein* which may indeed be related to it: *thryptein* means "to enfeeble," "to unman," "to hack to pieces." Euripides certainly intended the first meaning of the verb *tryphan*, "to be made effeminate"; he may also have meant the more literal meaning of *thryptein* as a sinister reference to the *sparagmos* to come.

This last utterance before Pentheus disappears holds Pentheus' joy in yielding at last to the delicious, luxury-hungry part of himself, in the same grip as his coming death by *sparagmos*. Both the pleasure which Dionysos grants and the fury he inflicts upon humankind are embodied in that word. More clearly than anything else in the play, the word *tryphan* defines the menace in the passive nature of the Dionysiac: as symbolized in *The Bakkhai*, to be a Dionysiac is to surrender to the sweet and terrible pressure pounding against and stripping away all the restraints the male ego can muster, which keep it from reveling in the sensual world a female at her most free imagines for herself. Probably no other symbolic act could have expressed the devastation Euripides saw in Dionysos. To lose your very sexual identity, to feel suddenly blossoming in your body a sexual awareness thought forever alien, is an event whose pleasure cannot be severed from its horror.

Whether Euripides offers this as an actual, rather than a symbolic definition of the Dionysiac cannot be finally settled by literary criticism. But this vision of the Dionysiac as what makes us "give in" adds something to our understanding of *The Bakkhai*. Intoxication by wine or blood, lust for both violence and infinite peace, union with god's power, loss of individuality, the death of thought, are all potential destinations when one surrenders. The disciplined strength of the rational mind collapses. As Nietzsche suggested in *The Birth of Tragedy*, the ultimate consequence of losing rational control is primal chaos, which has no history or order, where nothing has a name, and where the pain of rational control and order lies far away. In *The Bakkhai* that pain is presented to us by the steps through which Kadmos leads Agave back to consciousness, rebuilding name by name her recognition of her own calamity, and thus rebuilding order itself, her cosmos, from its dissolution into the madness and chaos which are the creations of Dionysos.

Structurally, Agave's return to sanity completes the action which began when Dionysos imposed madness on her and the other Theban women. In every sense her return to sanity is the exact opposite of the journey to Dionysian possession. It is painful, intellectual, reality-seeking, identity-seeking, and her cries are of devastating knowledge. The kind of cycle completed by the awakening of Agave is quite different from that defined by Aristotle, and which we expect to find in a Greek drama: a series of complications followed by an illuminating unravelling was Aristotle's perception of dramatic structure, a type found in some of Euripides' plays, most notably *Hippolytos,* but which is more evident in Sophocles and Aeschylus. We will, however, usually be frustrated if we look for Aristotelian structure in Euripides, even (and especially) in his finest plays. Instead of a plot in the ordinary sense we find that the essential action must be described in terms of a shift in our attitudes and sympathies. This kind of shift should also be distinguished from a movement common in modern literature which takes the reader or viewer through the development, maturation or decay of a central figure. It has often been remarked that except for rare cases (such as the education of Neoptolemos in Sophocles' *Philoctetes*), Greek dramas do not concern themselves with this kind of conscious growth. Yet, in the more characteristic Euripidean plays such as *The Bakkhai,* we do have a movement of an analogous sort. Euripides builds plays not so much on a shift in what the dramatic character understands, but on a shift in the *audience's* understanding of these characters. Euripides refuses to give us what modern readers and audiences look for—a sympathetic figure through whose eyes we can experience the actions of the play. In *The Bakkhai* our sympathies are not allowed to be attached permanently to any figure, not the god, or the king, or the king's mother. As a consequence the audience can accept more readily than it could in a modern plot a constant series of discoveries that it had been incomplete in its perception of the several characters.

The audience at first is fascinated with Dionysos' aloof cunning, and feels distaste for the blundering and sadistic Pentheus; then it moves toward sympathy for the doomed and mesmerized king, while it grows more and more repelled as the savage god reveals his nature. Agave, whom we glimpsed earlier only as a spiteful sister of Semelê, now draws our shock and pain for a mother unconsciously forced to butcher her son. Reinforcing this movement is the steady transformation of the Chorus' songs from celebration of sweetness and purifying revelation to ecstatic cries for brutal revenge. This change in the way we perceive the characters helps us to measure the thrill and utter disorientation of having the opposite sexual nature possess one's being. Ultimately the audience discovers that it was mistaken to think that divinity could long wear a human face and receive human admiration. It learns that mortal intelligence and emotions cannot cope with or even comprehend the violent extremes of the Bakkhic god. Such shocks to its perception of the characters guide its understanding of Euripides' bitter vision of an implacable divine presence not outside, but *within* our nature, a presence utterly hostile to what we uneasily call our humanity.

The Bakkhai may plunge us into a chaos of impulses, but Euripides has skillfully imposed a form on an action that would make no sense unless he assumed a totally healthy and ordered person: the audience or the reader of the play. This person must do the reverse of living in the mindless present, no matter how tempted by the choral odes and stunning descriptions. This reader must connect ideas and images in a hundred pregnant or alarming combinations; must listen to ironies undercut plausible speeches and hear the scream in the delicious lyrical outcry; must read the poetry with true *sophia* —wisdom responsive to both the Dionysian and rational lobes of the brain. Such a reader will note that the word "blessed" is used of both Agave holding Pentheus' severed head and by the Chorus early in the play as it recounts the pleasures of the initiate. The reader will connect Kadmos' healing questioning of Agave to Dionysos' destructive probing of Pentheus; see Pentheus' vanity and love of rage mirrored in that fury which the maenads love; and hear both the power of the Chorus' definition of *sophia*—and its madness.

> What is wisdom?
>   When the gods
> crush our enemies, their heads cowed
> under the hard fist of our power,
> that is glory!
>   —and glory
> always is the prize men crave.

*   *   *

I have followed the text and commentary of E. R. Dodds' remarkable edition of the play, and have departed from his guidance in a few instances only, the most significant of which are cited in the notes.

Recent translators of Greek drama into English verse have generally aimed at making translations that are loyal to both the literal text and to the natural speech rhythms of contemporary poetry. My ambition on this score does not differ from that of my colleagues.

In several respects translation must be a cumulative and a collaborative calling. When a previous translator found what seemed to me the right and inevitable English word to render a Greek one, I have borrowed and perpetuated it. In the years of work on this *Bakkhai* I have enjoyed a combative and exhilarating collaboration with my Hellenist and poet friends. For specific help and encouragement at crucial moments I thank Donald Junkins, James Hynd, Richard Wilbur, Robert Fitzgerald, Len Berkman and Sally Bagg, who has reminded me, as persistently but more gracefully than Pound's dictum, that poetry should be as well written as prose. I am indebted to Carol Schoen of the University of Massachusetts Press for her careful editing of the manuscript.

I began this translation while a Resident Fellow in 1969 at the National Translation Center in Austin, Texas, an institution which no longer exists and is therefore difficult to thank properly. The Classics department at Smith College provided a congenial occasion to test some of the interpretations presented in the introduction. Another less approving critic of the translation at earlier stages (whose identity is here held *in petto*) but whom I would also thank, has had a more beneficial influence than he might have imagined.

Thomas Gould and James Scully have helped me so generously with their friendship and their art, and so shared with me the obsessive passions of *The Bakkhai,* that if a *thiasos* of translation exists, we were one.

ROBERT BAGG
September 21, 1977
Northampton, Massachusetts

THE BAKKHAI

CHARACTERS   Dionysos

Chorus of Asian Bakkhai

Leader of the Chorus

Tiresias, a blind prophet

Kadmos, ex-king and founder of Thebes

Pentheus, young king of Thebes

Soldier

Herdsman

Messenger

Agave, daughter of Kadmos, mother of Pentheus

SCENE   *Before the royal palace at Thebes. Two doors open in the façade; a great one leads to the royal apartments, a rougher one to a stable which serves also as a jail. At center stage but near the main door is an altar and smouldering ruins of a house, both enclosed by a thick mesh of grapevines. This is Semelê's tomb. Dionysos enters. He is in his late teens, with curly long blond hair and a soft unmuscular body. He wears an ivy crown, a fawn or leopard skin cloak and carries a* thyrsos, *the long fennel stalk with ivy braided into its tip. His style is one of radiant, uncanny calm, but touched with sudden bursts of excitement and irony which hint at the fury to come.*

radiant
uncanny
calm

DIONYSOS I'm back!—a god standing on ground
where I was born, in Thebes.
Lightning ripped me
from the pregnant body
of Kadmos' daughter, Semelê.
That blast of flame was my midwife.
I am Dionysos, the son of Zeus.

You see me now at the rivers,
Dirce and Ismenus, but my godhead
you cannot see, because I've changed it   10
for *this:* the body of a man.
There—by the palace—is my mother's tomb:
the lightning girl.
Those glowing ruins were her house, once.
Now they're proof that the fire of Zeus
never dies down, proof that Hera—
still murderous
toward my mother—still rages
white hot under those ashes.
I'm pleased by what Kadmos has built   20
for his daughter: this tombsite,
a sacred place no one enters.
I wreathe it myself with clustering
green growing vines.

I first gave joy to the people
far from here, in the golden deserts
of Phrygia and Lydia.
Then I left, circling
over the Persian steppes
where blazing sun beats down,   30
past Baktrian fortress towns
and the Medes' gale-brewing wastes.
I crossed lucky Arabia
to the salt sea, where I found
a great mix of Levantines and Greeks—
who rub shoulders the length of that swarming
Mediterranean coast, and who pack
towering seaports with the crush of life.
Everywhere on my march here
I taught my holy dances, my mysteries,   40
and everywhere, the people knew I was god.

From Asia I came on to Thebes,
my first Greek city, to make shrill

"shrill barbarian joy"

barbarian joy flare up in her women.
I bound fawnskin to their bodies,
armed them all with my green fennel wand—
in battle it's an ivied spear.

My purpose is to end the lies
told by Semelê's own sisters,
who had least right to speak them.   50
They swore to Thebes that Zeus was not
my father, that some man she'd loved
made Semelê pregnant, and that her claim
Zeus fathered her child was a gamble
Kadmos forced her to take—
a blasphemy, her sisters crowed,
which made Zeus in a flash of rage
crush out her life.

Semelê's sisters lied, now they suffer.
My frenzy touched their minds, it drives them   60
outdoors, to roam the mountains
dressed in my sacred gear,
stupefied by my power.

punishing the women

I've emptied Thebes of her women,
but only her women,
and I control their madness.
They perch high up on the bare rocks,
the well-born and the dirt poor—
a pack that Kadmos' own daughters join
under the blue-green pines.   70

Like it or not, this town
must learn to perfection
all my mysteries have to teach.
When the shock of my power
dawns on its people, they will believe:
that my mother was honest
and that I am the god she bore to Zeus.

vengeful →

By now the old king, Kadmos, has given up
his throne and its honors to his grandson:
Pentheus, a young man spoiling   80
to fight gods, who picks me as the god
he would like most to challenge.
He spills wine offerings to some gods
but excludes *me* from that honor.
Nor does he speak the name
"Dionysos" in his prayers.

Therefore: what happens next
will be my demonstration—
to him and to Thebes—that I was born a god.
When my worship here runs smoothly   90
I'll move on—to surprise some other
country with my divinity.

Should Thebes turn against me, by sending troops
to sweep my Bakkhai off the mountain—I'll
face their army in battle,
my own maenads raging at my back.

But to make my plans work
I need this human disguise—Thebes
must think I'm a man.

Let's go! my   100
women who adore me!
After following me across Asia,
down Tmolus, the mountain wall
that guards Lydia, and after sharing
my marches and my rests,
you're part of me!
Give me the drums
Goddess Rhea and I
taught you to beat in Phrygia—
there's the palace: pound the drums!   110
Hound Pentheus with your booms!
Turn the whole city
out to watch.
                    Meanwhile
climbing straight up
Cithaeron's ravines,
I'll overtake my Bakkhai
dancing on the heights—
I'll run them
wild with ecstasy!   120

(Dionysos runs off. The Chorus enters chanting, shaking
tamborines, clapping them to a stirring beat. They wear
fawnskins, ivy garlands, and carry the long wands of
fennel.)

CHORUS   We ran down Tmolus, our holy mountain
          and crossed Asia, moving fast
          to do sweet work for the God Who Cries Out—
          all the labor we give him, he gives back

as joy!—roared out
in our dances so lightly run
    to Bakkhos!

Who's with us
    out here in the streets?
Who's there   130
    in the dark house?
Come! All of you! Keep your
mouths quiet and your minds pure.
Hear us sing
    to Dionysos the living god
truths that will never die.

Bless the man, bless his luck,
who learns the mysteries of god:
he lives in sacred joy.

Bless the dancers   140
who give body and soul to Bakkhos!
We take them
with us into the holy body of god.
Bakkhos will dance
steep mountain joy into our spirits
until we are pure.
We keep Great Mother Kybele's rites—
twisting the ivy into our hair,
lifting the green wand
to Dionysos our god.   150

Go out
into the hills, Bakkhai! Find him!
Bring home the God Who Cries Out,
down from the Phrygian hills.
Find dancing room for the Zeuschild
through the wide streets of Greece.
Bring the god home whose mother
suffered the lightning's
brutal contractions,
which drove the foetus out of her body—   160
but Zeus, with a god's quick hand,
opens his own thigh, recovers his son,
then shuts with golden pins
his flesh over Bakkhos.

Hera never saw him, but the Fates did—
the child grew ripe in their care, till Zeus

gave birth to his bull-horned son,
the god, and crowned him with serpents.
From that time to ours
all god-maddened women   170
wear earthcrawling snakes in their hair.

Thebans,
weave ivy through your hair
for Semelê, whom you raised.
Bright berries and bryony flowers
will burst you all into bloom.
Pick sprigs from the oak and fir,
tuft your brown skins of fawn
with soft white wool—
these will put you in mind   180
of Bakkhos.

Guard the violence in your green wand,
respect its holy power.
This land will be dancing
when god runs his pack
out to the mountain, pulling the women
free of their looms,
their minds stung wild
by Bakkhos.

We honor you,   190
holy island of Crete
where Zeus was born,
we salute you, Kuretes,
who raised him
in your black caves—
there the dancing Korybantes
first stretched
resilient hide over drums
and struck
the tense beat of Bakkhos—   200
they blew the flute's
sweet piercing voice
to lift and lighten the beat,
then handed on
that beating drum
to Rhea, our goddess mother,
who taught it to carry
the joysongs of maenads—

but raving satyrs
captured the drum,   210
now it beats through
their orgies, which Dionysos
delights in, every other year.

The mountain goes sweet with Bakkhos!
He's there in the maenad,
his fawnskin's on her body—
out of the running pack
she drops to the earth!
She kills in blood, she devours in joy
the raw flesh of a goat, and is hurled   220
back to the mountains
of Phrygia and Lydia,
cried on by the Loud God, whose cry
runs through her.

the maenad embodies Bakkhos

Beneath her the meadow is running with milk
running with wine
running slowly
with the nektar of bees.

And the man turned god!
Turned Bakkhos himself!   230
holds up the flaming pine
whose smoke
is Syrian incense,
running and wavering
he floats
red sparks and milky smoke behind him,
his great voice
fires the stragglers,
roaring his strength into them—
then shakes his airy curls   240
in the mountain wind.

His shout thunders over
the maenads' cries
of rising joy:
"Faster, my Bakkhai!
you glitter again
with gold that pours
down our mountain—
dance the god's dances,
pound the god's drum.   250
Pour glory on him!

The joy in your voices
swells up
through his booming voice—
yell out the wild Phrygian cry!"

Lotus flutes whistle their sweet holy notes,
the running women veer in their flight
to the mountain!
To the mountain!

Waves of joy shake the maenad— 260
like a colt grazing near its mare
nimble and skittering
she breaks leaping away.

*(Tiresias enters, a white-bearded blind prophet in Bakkhic
dress. He carries a green wand which he uses to test his way.
His voice bellows.)*

TIRESIAS   Who's in charge of these gates? Find me Kadmos,
Agenor's son! That immigrant from Sidon
who built Thebes her stone battlements.
Tell him Tiresias is waiting. He'll know why.
We're both old men, but we've said
we'll do it—now we will: dress in fawnskins,
tie ourselves green wands of ivy 270
and crown our heads with its tendrils.

*(Kadmos emerges from the palace. He, too, wears Dionysos'
ritual garb.)*

KADMOS   Dear old friend!
That voice! Even indoors
I knew it was yours: a voice
wise as the man.
So here I am,
committed to Bakkhos, wearing his gear.
My daughter had a son who's now a god.
We'll do our part to enlarge his power.
Tiresias, you're wise enough to know where 280
god's people are dancing—instruct me,
one old man to another.
We'll go there! —
tossing our heads, making the grey hair fly.
We'll never tire—not if we leap and whirl
all night, then spend the whole next day
drumming the ground with our green wands.
It's pure joy to forget how old I am.

TIRESIAS	I feel the same—young and ready to dance.
KADMOS	Shall we ride a chariot into the hills?

290

TIRESIAS	No! That would not show respect for the god. We'd better go out there on foot.
KADMOS	Then let me guide you, old man, I'll lead you like a child.
TIRESIAS	No, Bakkhos will move us with easy strides.
KADMOS	Who else in Thebes will dance for Bakkhos?
TIRESIAS	No one else. We're two sane men in a mad city.
KADMOS	Then let's not linger *here!* Take my hand.
TIRESIAS	You take mine, friend. We're well matched.
KADMOS	I know what I am—a man who must die. I can't afford to take any god lightly.

(margin, handwritten: to dance is sane)

300

TIRESIAS	You won't hear me asking which gods exist or cross-examining their actions. I hold with those hardy traditions we inherit from our fathers— their roots go deep, they're old as time. The wisest man living, though he brings to bear his keenest logic, will never break their grip on our lives.

310

(margin, handwritten: not too old to dance)

Now this ivy in my hair will shock those
who think old men should act their age.
But Bakkhos has no law which says
that young men must dance and old men can't dance—
this god excludes no one. He wants honor
from each of us, he wants our joy,
all we can give him.

KADMOS	Tiresias, because you're blind, I'll be your eyes.

                   I see
Pentheus coming here in a hurry, Echion's boy,
in whose hands I put the power of Thebes.
He looks upset, there must be news.

320

*(Pentheus enters. He, too, is in his late teens, quick and
assured of mind and body. Friends and servants accompany
him. He does not notice Tiresias and Kadmos for some
time.)*

(margin, handwritten: who is really blind)

PENTHEUS The crisis broke while I was abroad. Word reached me
that something new and evil is at work here.
It harms our women, who desert their families
to prowl out there in the mountain forests.
They claim possession by Bakkhos, the sudden god—
is he a god?—whom they worship with a lewd
hypnotic dance. Packs of these women
drink wine from brimming bowls, then creep off   330
to isolated nooks where they give sex
freely to any lusty male who wants them.
They exalt this activity by calling it
a maenad's offering to the new god Bakkhos,
but it's pure Aphrodite they adore.
I have arrested a handful already,
they're tied up now in the public stable
out of harm's way. My next move
will be to track down the women
still out there on the mountain   340
and drag them back in iron nets.
That should end with dispatch
this outbreak of Bakkhos.

A stranger, they tell me, has slipped into town,
a smooth-talking spellbinder, from Lydia,
with long curly blond hair. And it's *perfumed!*
He's rosy-cheeked, and his bright insinuating eyes
promise our women more of Aphrodite's joy
than they can stand. Day and night he bothers them,
he dangles his rituals and they swarm to him.   350
But once he's penned in my jail
I'll have his head cut from his body,
his wand will stop its pounding,
his tossing hair will lie still.
This stranger tells us Dionysos is a god,
a 'god' that Zeus—supposedly—
carried in his thigh. Here's the truth:
he's a 'god' lightning burned up with his mother
as punishment for her great lie—
that she had slept with Zeus.   360
No matter who this stranger is,
we should hang him for blasphemy.

*(Pentheus at last notices Kadmos and Tiresias
who have been listening to him with amazement.)*

Now that is a remarkable sight!

Tiresias,
the master of portents, in a spotted fawnskin.
Grandfather Kadmos—should we all laugh? —
dancing, parading with a wand! It's painful
to watch old men go soft in the head.
Please, Grandfather, take the ivy off.
Drop the wand.   370
Tiresias!
All this must be your work.
You promote a new god to our people
in order to get rich—by selling
bird prophecies and prodding the future
from the organs of burning beasts.
If you weren't such a weak old man
I'd lock you in the stable with the Bakkhai
for sponsoring their filthy rituals.
Show me a bowl foaming with wine   380
among feasting women—and I'll show you proof
nothing's healthy in that festival.

LEADER   That's blasphemy! You are sneering at the gods,
Pentheus, and at Kadmos, who sowed the snaketeeth
which shot up into men. Why does Echion's son
want to humiliate his own people?

TIRESIAS   When a wise man takes hold of a valid case
we expect him to argue well. Now your tongue
is lively, you sound impressive, but something's
missing: intelligence. You talk nonsense.   390
A man who persuades us because his speech
is poised and aggressive, is a civic
menace when he lacks judgment.
Now the new god you laugh at—
his future power throughout Greece will be vast,
I can't even predict myself how vast.
Young fellow,
mankind is blessed with two supreme natural powers:
Earth power and Liquid power. Demeter,
or Goddess Earth—call her whichever you like—   400
gave us our dry life-nourishing bread.
Another god then came to complete her good work:
Semelê's child Bakkhos,
who found a vital juice in the grape cluster—
wine!—when men drink their fill, it stops grief
by drowning the day's troubles in sleep.

How else could we ease the ache of living?
What's more, we sprinkle drops of this god
to summon other gods when we need their help.
Always, the good life flows through Bakkhos.   410
     Now, from this god, the truth of prophecy
speaks—for the ecstasy of maenads and the madman's
delirium are both visionary.
When Bakkhos comes rushing into their bodies
they're raving mad, but what they say comes true.
In wartime, Bakkhos even gives Ares a hand.
Picture an army aligned for battle.
Suddenly it panics, men drop their weapons and run
before a single spear has been thrown.
That swift fever of dread is also Bakkhos.   420
I promise you, Dionysos will climb Delphi! Someday
you will see him leap and his maenad packs
racing across the high ground between crags,
carrying pine torches and the sacred wand.
O I think Bakkhos will succeed in Greece!
Believe me, Pentheus, don't be so sure
that brute force is what governs human life.
Your mind is riddled with sick fantasies
which you act on as though they made sense.
You would do better to welcome this god.   430
Open the gates. Pour wine in his honor.
Learn his dances, wear his crown.
As for that point which upsets you
the most—sex: Dionysos will not suppress
lust in a woman: her own character must.
Even at the peak of Bakkhic abandon
a chaste woman remains perfectly chaste.
Now, when the whole city turns out to praise you,
Pentheus, doesn't that lift your spirits?
Try to grasp that this god also loves praise.   440
Therefore, Kadmos and I, though it makes
you laugh, will put his ivy on and dance.
Pair of old fools? No doubt. But dance we must,
by god we'll dance! I will not cross a god
no matter what arguments you bully me with.
You have a raging brain fever—and no drug
will cure it. But I think something will.

LEADER   Tiresias, you are Apollo's prophet,
but he'll agree with you—that Bakkhos
is no less powerful a god.   450

[handwritten margin notes: "truth in madness" and "what will?"]

KADMOS   You listen to Tiresias, son. He's right.
Don't turn your back on our fathers' ways—
stay here with us. Collect your wits—and start
thinking like a king. Suppose it's true
that Bakkhos is no real god—
proclaim him one. It's a fine distinguished lie!
Our Semelê then becomes a god's mother,
a cult will honor her, and her good luck
will shower prestige on our whole family.
Remember how your cousin Actaeon died.   460
Out there, on those same wooded hillsides,
he told the world he could outhunt Artemis.
His own man-eating hounds ripped him apart.
Something like that might happen to you.
Don't let it.
                 Here, I'll crown you with ivy.
We'll honor this god of ours together.

PENTHEUS   *Don't touch me with that crown!* Go out there,
wallow in Bakkhos yourself. But don't smear
your crazy squalor off on me. Your folly   470
I will punish at its source: this teacher of yours.
Men, go at once to where this prophet
cuts open birds. Take iron poles and rock
his altar over on its side. Smash it.
Leave his whole operation rubble.
Scatter his holy ribbons
into the teeth of the wind—that will rip
the old prophet where it hurts.
The rest of you patrol the town and drag back
the stranger with a girlish body—the one who   480
inflames and corrupts all our women.
When you've caught him, lash his hands, lead him here.
I have his sentence ready: we'll stone him
to death. He'll be stunned when he finds out
how we Thebans celebrate Bakkhos.

TIRESIAS   Crazy fool! You don't know what your words risk.
Did I say you were mindless? That's wrong.
You're a maniac. Kadmos, pray for this boy.
However savage he is, we'll pray that god
has no evil surprise for Thebes.   490
Pick up your wand, we'll leave.
We'll travel holding each other up, because
two stumbling old men make a shameful sight.
But we'll accept what comes. Let Bakkhos,

son of Zeus, know we are his slaves.
                                    Kadmos,
Pentheus' name means grief—
take care he doesn't force
that grief on your own flesh and blood.
That's not my prophecy, that's common sense.   500
When that fool speaks, his folly shouts.

*(Tiresias and Kadmos leave on the road toward Cithaeron.
Pentheus goes into the palace.)*

CHORUS   Lady Holiness, even among gods
you are a power,
a queen,
and the dark beat of your gold wings
wheeling
sends a chill over the earth.

Did you hear Pentheus
sneer at the Loud One?—
his insolence   510
does this to Semelê's child,
who, when the Blessed gather to feast,
their shoulders in roses,
lavender bloom on their hair,
    see our god
for what he is: a Prince!
With open hands he gives us
mountain dancing, joy
that makes us whole,
flutes running with laughter,   520
and wine that puts an end
to all our troubles, wine
flashing, pouring out
wherever the gods feast.
There the ivy dancers
coming to rest, drink sleep
from the swirling bowl.

A reckless mouth and a mad
defiant mind
             ruin a man—   530
but restraint and good sense
protect him: though far off
in the brilliant sky,
the gods watch us:
cleverness is not wisdom,

nor is the flash of pride
that tempts mankind out of its depth.
Life passes so fast—
knowing that, who would chase
greatness, and lose the sweet life   540
already in our hands?
Men die on the track
of such glory—but I call
what they do madness.

If only I were there
        on Cyprus
Aphrodite's island,
where little Loves,
        calling
        dance, dance!   550
distract us all day long.
Take me to the town
        of Paphos
where no rain falls,
but the far-off
barbarian Nile
with its hundred mouths
washes the Paphian shore
until she breeds green life.

Take me to charmed   560
        Pieria, where
on the foothills of Olympos
        the Muses live.
Take me to the home
        of the Graces,
        to the woods
where Desire runs—there
when you dance, god's in you,
        your voice roars,
it summons him, the God Who   570
Cries Out! to your joy.
Let's go where the wild dance
is loved, let's go where it's welcome!

Our god delights
in festive good times,
but he loves also
Peace, who makes men rich
and saves the young men's lives.

He gives wine freely
To the powerful, to the poor.
its pleasure
drowns all their pain.   580

But god hates any man
who does not fill his nights
with pleasure, his days with calm.
Watch out
for the arrogant thinker:
he's dangerous,
he never lets up. ⇥

I believe only   590
what common men of plain good sense
believe: anything they do
I will do.

*(Enter Soldier with bound Dionysos; Pentheus emerges
from palace.)*

SOLDIER   He's some fierce beast you made us hunt,
Pentheus! We caught him with no trouble.
He went tame on us, wouldn't run,
just held his wrists out—like this.
                                No sign
of fear in that rosy wine-drinker's face.
He smiled as we tied him up,   600
advising me at every step.
"Lead me to Pentheus," he said.
He made our work very easy.
I was ashamed, and told him, "Stranger,
Pentheus ordered your arrest. Blame him.
I carry out the order, but I don't like it."
There's something else. Those captured madwomen
you chained in the stable—they're free, they're dancing
back up the mountain, chasing their loud god.
All the shackles let go of their ankles,   610
the locked bolts loosened and dropped off the doors
with no blow from any human hand.
That stranger brings so many miracles to Thebes
he overflows with them. Now he's all your worry.

PENTHEUS   Untie him—let him test our net if he wants.
He's fast—but is he faster than I am?
I don't think so.

(Pentheus silently examines Dionysos.)

Your body's not bad looking, Stranger—
to women, at least. That's the real point,
isn't it, of your trip to Thebes?   620
Of course it is: look at this wavy hair
at your cheeks. *I'm lovely,* it says, *Touch me!*
I don't think wrestling is your sport.
Nor did your creamy skin just happen.
You hid it from the sun, to save its pale beauty
for hunting Aphrodite in the dark.
(Belligerently.) Who are you? Born where?

DIONYSOS   No famous place.
Have you heard of Tmolus,
the mountain covered with flowers?   630

PENTHEUS   I know that its stone arms
ring the town of Sardis.

DIONYSOS   Now you know where I'm from:
the Lydian mountains.

PENTHEUS   Who ordered these rituals of yours into Greece?

DIONYSOS   Bakkhos, the child of Zeus,
delivers them himself.

PENTHEUS   So Lydia has its own version of Zeus
to father its bastard gods?

DIONYSOS   There is only one Zeus: the god who loved Semele.   640

PENTHEUS   Were you dreaming when god possessed you?
Or face to face?

DIONYSOS   Face to face—
with a god who gave me ritual power.

PENTHEUS   Tell me about these mysteries of yours.

DIONYSOS   I couldn't tell *you.* You're not one of *us.*

PENTHEUS   What does this ritual do—I mean
for those who join it?

DIONYSOS   We keep that knowledge to ourselves.
But it's worth having.   650

PENTHEUS   You tell me nothing with so much cunning
it makes me ache to hear more.

DIONYSOS   The wild dances of this god punish disbelievers.

PENTHEUS   You've seen the god up close—what is he like?

DIONYSOS   That's not for *me* to say. He can look like—anyone.

PENTHEUS   You start to say something
but your words lead nowhere.

DIONYSOS   True wisdom stupefies a fool.

PENTHEUS   Is Thebes the first place you've brought this god?

DIONYSOS   No, our dancing joy has swept Asia.   660

PENTHEUS   Asians aren't Greeks—what do they know?

DIONYSOS   This time, they've caught on much faster than you.
They respond differently to life.

PENTHEUS   These rituals—do they happen in daylight? Or at night?

DIONYSOS   Mostly at night. Darkness helps us to feel holy.

PENTHEUS   You mean it helps you to rape women.

DIONYSOS   A worse outrage
can happen in broad daylight.

PENTHEUS   You'll pay dearly for that cynical wit.

DIONYSOS   Provoking god, you'll find, exacts its own price.   670

PENTHEUS   For someone dressed like a mild
priest of Bakkhos, you talk remarkably tough.
But it's all talk.

DIONYSOS   Then what will you do
to punish me? Will it be savage?

PENTHEUS   First, I'll cut off your sweet curls.

DIONYSOS   My hair is divine—I grow it for god.

(Pentheus supervises his men, who cut off Dionysos' curls.)

PENTHEUS   Give me that wand.

DIONYSOS   Take it yourself: it's the wand Dionysos uses.

(Pentheus seizes the wand.)

PENTHEUS   Now we can drive you down to the stable,   680
bolt it, and post guards.

DIONYSOS   When I wish to go free
god will turn me loose.

PENTHEUS — Then go rally your Bakkhai *now*,
whip them into a frenzy yelling for Bakkhos.

DIONYSOS — He is so close, he sees
what I suffer with his own eyes.

PENTHEUS — Then why can't I see him? Where is this god?

DIONYSOS — Where I am. You can't see him
because you have no faith.   690

PENTHEUS — I've seen enough of your contempt. So has Thebes.
Take him.

DIONYSOS — Men, don't use force on me.
Don't offend wisdom
to obey that blind fool.

PENTHEUS — And I say: chain him! You have no power,
you're not in command here. I am.

DIONYSOS — Why, you're not even in command
of your own life!
You don't know   700
what you are doing, or who you are.

PENTHEUS — I am Pentheus, son of Echion and Agave.

DIONYSOS — No, *sorrow* is what your name means,
Pentheus. And *pain*. It fits.

PENTHEUS — Move him out, lock him in a horse stall—
he'll find enough darkness down there
for the kind of dancing he likes so much.
As for your women accomplices, who help you
carry out this evil nightmare, I've just
made them my slaves.   710
I might sell them,
or I might work them at my palace looms.
But I'll have peace. No more drums!
No more stamping feet.

DIONYSOS — I'm ready. I'll go now—
though I cannot be hurt
by an act which cannot take place.
But you, Pentheus, can be certain
that the god you call "dead"—
is Dionysos, a god so real   720
he'll make you answer for every

outrage you do him. Insofar
as your ropes punish me,
they punish also him, the living god.

(Soldiers escort Dionysos off; Pentheus follows.)

CHORUS Queen Dirce,
child of the great river
Achelaus—are you still
the charming rivergirl
who bathed our god?
Cleansing the foetus   730
Zeus fathered,
the son he pulled from his own
      everblazing fire,
        and as he did, cried:

"Dithyrambos, my son!
     Live here
in my male womb.
I name you *Bakkhos*—
     Thebans
will know you by that name."   740

Now tell us, Dirce,
why you shun us, and turn your back
when we dance on your banks!
We bring you maenads wearing flowers,
and still you tell us: No,
still you slide coolly away.

But as sure as there is
      pleasure in grapes
Bakkhos presses into wine,
your neglect of the God   750
Who Cries Out
    will end:
          and soon.

There is evil in Pentheus' blood—
the bestial earth blazes in his face,
an inhuman snake-face
like those his giant fathers had,
those butchers who were beaten
when they tried to fight gods.

He's a crude beast: *we*   760
are the god's servants,

yet we are the ones
Pentheus wants to enslave.
He's thrown our companion,
shackled, into a dark cell.

Dionysos, son of Zeus—
how can you stand to watch
this bully using force
against us, your teachers of joy?
Come down from Olympos, Lord,   770
armed with your wand
flashing gold—
stop his abuse,
end his murdering days.

Where are you?
Loud One!
Somewhere on Nysa
the beast-loving mountain, leading
packs of maenads with your wand?
Or running the Corycian highlands?   780
Or gone to the vast woods on Olympos
where Orpheus once
plucking music from his lyre
moved the trees! moved the wild beasts!
spellbound
toward his singing.

Now the god turns to you
graceful Pieria,
he dances down your slopes
to join his Bakkhic enjoyers—   790
he splashes across
fastflowing Axios,
he's driving his maenads
on over Lydias,
the riverfather
who makes men rich, makes them happy,
whose waters carry gold,
making that land of fast horses
        glow.

(An earthquake. Blasts of lightning.)

DIONYSOS *(Gives a great yell.)*
Hear me, Bakkhai!   800
Bakkhai!
Do you hear my shout?

CHORUS   *(Speaking individually.)*
—Whose voice are we hearing?
—Where is it coming from?
—Is it you, Loud One?
—The god who comes when we call
now calls for us!

DIONYSOS   *(Another yell.)*
The son of Zeus, the son of Semelê
calls you now!

CHORUS   —Lord, we are here.   810
—Master, come down,
be with us! Loud One!

DIONYSOS   Poseidon, tear the earth!
Break up the world's floor, here, now!

CHORUS   —The palace totters, it's going down!
—Look, its front cracks, it's splitting open!
—Dionysos is in there. I feel him.
—Worship him, adore him!
—O I do! I do!
—Watch those columns! They've   820
broken loose from the roof.
—The Loud One is roaring
his great roar of triumph!

DIONYSOS   Lightning, strike this place!
Burn Pentheus' palace to the ground.
Burn it!

CHORUS   Look! Fire blazes up
over Semelê's tomb,
where she was killed by Zeus!—
that's the lightning that killed her!   830
Flat on the ground, Maenads.
Bakkhos is coming! The son of Zeus!
He's left the high soaring palace
rubble lying crushed in a field.

*(The Chorus falls face down. Dionysos reappears disguised
still as his own priest, now in an openly exhilarated mood.)*

DIONYSOS   You lovely terrified Bakkhai from Asia!
What knocked you down? Rise up,
take heart. The panic is over.
That was *Bakkhos* who sent the earthquake
rolling through Pentheus' palace.

LEADER   It's you! You light up our holy lives   840
with joy when you shout like a god!
You'll save us now, but without you
we were alone and defenseless.
To see you unharmed is a great relief.

DIONYSOS   You must have been sunk in gloom
when they hauled me into that stable.

LEADER   How could we help it? Who could protect us
while you were locked in that jail?
How did you escape that godless man?

DIONYSOS   I freed myself. Gently, without exertion.   850

LEADER   Didn't he lash ropes around your arms?

DIONYSOS   He did, convinced he had me in his grip.
He tied me up, though, without
touching me—hallucination
fed his desires. That
was how I humiliated him.
Down in the stables where he led me
a bull faced him—he roped it, thinking
the bull was me, hauling on the noose
that held the bull's hooves and knees,   860
breathing hard, raging, drenched
with sweat, his teeth grinding into his lip.
I sat and quietly watched. Then Bakkhos
came from nowhere, he rocked the building,
he blew flames back to life
on his mother's tomb—
the palace seemed to catch fire—
but it burned in *his* mind only.
He scrambled here, raced there, screaming for water,
for bucketfuls of River—which his slaves brought   870
until the palace was awash with confusion.
Then Pentheus quit fighting fire
to chase me, hacking with his dark sword
after me through the palace. The God Who
Cries Out obliged him—maybe this happened,
I could have imagined it—
by shining a phantom ME out in the courtyard.
Pentheus lunged at it, murdering this man-sized glow
which sparkled as he cut what seemed to be my throat.
Not yet satisfied, Dionysos humbled him   880
once more: he smashed the palace into dust—

the fool's reward for jailing me. Exhausted,
Pentheus dropped his blade and collapsed.
He's a *man*, that's all. And he tried to fight god.
I was calm when I went outside to find you.
Pentheus' fury ceased to concern me.
Now I hear boots tramping—
he's about to come through that door
gasping with rage. But I'll deal with him calmly—
a cool head and an even temper   890
are indispensable to a wise man.

(Pentheus appears, dazed, in the palace doorway.)

PENTHEUS   Something horrible had me in there.
The stranger's gone—where?
He was chained!
Look! There he is.
Why are you here?
Why aren't you back inside?

DIONYSOS   You're staggering with rage. Stand still, calm down.

PENTHEUS   How did you do that—escape me?
What happened to your chains?   900

DIONYSOS   I told you—next time, listen—
that I'd be set free by someone.

PENTHEUS   Who? I can't keep up with all your
sudden explanations. Who?

DIONYSOS   The god who taught men to use grapes.

PENTHEUS   Put men on the towers and seal off the city.

DIONYSOS   I'm not impressed. Gods hurdle over walls.

PENTHEUS   You are clever—everywhere except where it counts.

DIONYSOS   That is just where my cleverness counts the most.

(Dionysos looks offstage at the Herdsman approaching.)

This man brings you news from the mountain.
Listen to him. And don't be anxious   910
about us: we won't run. We're here to stay.

(A young Herdsman enters from Cithaeron.)

HERDSMAN   Pentheus, Master of Thebes,
I live on Cithaeron where it snows
bright flurries the year round . . .

PENTHEUS   If you have news, Herdsman, tell it.

HERDSMAN   I've seen those holy women who ran
half-naked and frantic out of your gates,
covering ground like a flight of spears.
I've come down to tell you, and Thebes,   920
that what your women are doing in the hills
outstrips miracles, it's so strange, so horrible!
Will I be safe telling you the whole story?
Or should I cut it short? Pentheus,
you're an impatient master, who might
flare up at a man whose news you hated.
They say you can get angry like a king.

PENTHEUS   Speak freely. There's no need to fear me,
I don't punish innocent people.
But the more evil I hear about those maenads   930
the harder I'll be on *him*—that man there—all
their vile magic comes from him.

HERDSMAN   The sun had just come up, burning the chill
off the mountain pastures. My cattle were climbing
through steep rock country, when I spot
three packs of those dancing women—
Autonoë led one, your mother, Agave,
led the second, the third was Ino's—
all sleeping where exhaustion dropped them:
some with their backs leaning on fir boughs,   940
or their heads resting on piles of oak leaves.
No question they were carefree, king, but not vulgar,
not drunk, as you told it—or with sex in mind.
They weren't led through the woods by love-flutes.
Your mother Agave heard my cows lowing—
she stood up yelling
over her sleepers a great holy cry
to wake them up: their bodies shivered, they rubbed
their eyes until the bloom of sleep was gone,
then jumped up lightly to their full height—   950
old women, young women, and girls
not yet married—all moving
in perfect formation.
                         My god it was eerie.
First, they loosened their hair
down their backs and hitched their fawnskins up,
if the straps had slipped overnight.
                                        Then I saw,

like belts around each woman, *live snakes*
who twisted up to lick their cheeks!   960
And mothers whose new babies were back home
eased their aching breasts by picking up
gazelles and wild wolf cubs to suckle
with white human milk.
                                        Soon they were working
leaf-garlands into each other's hair—
of ivy, oak and bryony flowers.
                                   Then one struck her wand
to a rock—out jumps icy springwater!
Another pushed hers gently into the pasture   970
feeling for Bakkhos—she found the god
who made wine flood up right there!
Women eager for milk raked the meadow
with their fingers until it oozed out
fresh and white.
                          Raw honey was dripping
in sweet threads from their wands.
Had you been there watching, Pentheus,
you would have dropped to your knees
blessing this god you've been cursing.   980
We herdsmen met to trade miracles
all morning. We'd listen amazed, or outdo
each other's stories if we could.
                                      Then a drifter
who had learned how to talk fast in the city
saw his chance: "Listen, you mountain men," he said,
"if we hunt down Agave, the king's mother,
pull her clear of that dancing mob, Pentheus
will credit us with a great favor."
Good plan—or so it seemed then. We tunneled   990
through underbrush, elbowing up for an ambush.
At a signal from somewhere, the maenads
lifted their wands, dancing and chanting
Iakkhos, Child of Zeus, O God Who Cries Out,
their voices swelling together, then the whole
mountain started to dance for Bakkhos,
even the wild birds and squirrels filled with god
as they rushed past, shrilling for joy!
When Agave leaps my way, I scramble from my bush
grappling for her, but she shouts,   1000
"Over here! Sisters! My baying pack!
Men are hunting us! We'll fight them
with our wands!"

                                        If we hadn't run hard
they would have torn us apart.
Armed with nothing but their bare hands
they charged into the midst of our cattle
who were chewing grass in a peaceful meadow.
You could see one girl hold by the legs
ripped halves of a shrieking heifer,   1010
others tore into cows, sending cleft hooves
and rib-clusters spinning out into the trees
which caught shredded flesh and dripped blood.
Even some proud stud bulls
whose rage boiled under their horns, stumbled
and sank when the girls attacked—
a blur of hands, you couldn't count them all,
stripped off their coats of hide and flesh
faster than you could shut your royal eyes,
sir.   1020
          Then they ran so fast, they flew,
lifted like birds over the valley,
skimming the wheat along the river Asopus.
They landed on those villages in the foothills,
Hysia and Erythrae, like enemy raiders
grabbing everything—even children
from their homes.
                        What they stole stuck to their backs—
ironware, bronze—nothing fell to the ground.
Fire sizzled and flashed in their hair,   1030
but they weren't burned.
                              The mountain people were enraged.
They rushed for their weapons and waded in.
What happened was awful, hard to believe.
How could the men's tough sharp spears
not draw blood from a single maenad?—
while the women, hurling their green wands,
wounded the men until they turned tail and ran.
Men beaten by females!—but I think some god
helped the women.   1040
                        Now the maenads headed back
to the springs where they woke—those springs
Bakkhos set flowing, and they scrubbed
the blood off. Snakes licked the gore
crusted over their cheeks
until the maenads' faces glowed.

King, whoever this god is, welcome him.

Give him the city. He has power—*of all kinds*—
but his great strength is wine that cures heartache.
Lose wine, and we'd lose the love goddess next—   1050
we'd lose it all—whatever gives men joy.

(Exit Herdsman.)

LEADER
Truth isn't what this tyrant wants to hear—
I'm shaking—but he must be told:
No god is greater than Dionysos!

PENTHEUS
Here comes the Bakkhic savagery, raging,
out of control, burning its way here.
Now it's close. If we don't act now
Greece will look at us with disgust.
Soldier! Muster our heavy infantry
outside the Elektran Gates. Commit   1060
our horsemen, the fastest we have.
Hold ready the light infantry
and the long-range archers.
Thebes, we're going to war against the Bakkhai!
I've had enough. We are humiliated
when we let women act like this.

DIONYSOS
Pentheus, you'll reject my advice,
but even though you wrong me, I'll
warn you again: don't use force against a god.
Keep the peace. The Loud One won't let you   1070
clear his maenads off that mountain—
too much joy is echoing all over it.

PENTHEUS
Don't lecture me and don't provoke me.
You're free now. Keep this up and you won't be.

DIONYSOS
If I were a man enraged at a god—as you are—
I'd call off my rebellion. Why don't you
make a sacrifice to this god?

PENTHEUS
I'll burn him an offering—one he deserves—
the corpses of his women, after I myself
have made the bloodiest slaughter   1080
Cithaeron has ever seen.

DIONYSOS
You will all run terrified for your lives.
The maenads' wands wave your bronze shields aside.

PENTHEUS
This stranger wears me down. No matter who holds
the upper hand, he never shuts his mouth.

DIONYSOS	Friend, there is still time to make peace.
PENTHEUS	How? By letting female slaves dictate to me?
DIONYSOS	I'll lead your women home unharmed.
PENTHEUS	You're damned shrewd!—talking me into some trap.
DIONYSOS	What trap? My shrewdness could be your salvation.
PENTHEUS	I think you and your maenads plot no end of Bakkhic joy.
DIONYSOS	No, that is something that I plot with god.
PENTHEUS	Bring my weapons. You—we're through talking.
DIONYSOS	Are we! Would you like to see maenads sitting together, up there on the mountain?
PENTHEUS	I would give all the gold I have to see that.
DIONYSOS	So, suddenly you're passionate to see them?
PENTHEUS	If they were drunk, I wouldn't like that. But . . .
DIONYSOS	But you'd enjoy it, though it hurt you to see it?
PENTHEUS	I would. I'll keep quiet and watch from a pine.
DIONYSOS	They'll corner you, no matter how softly you sneak up.
PENTHEUS	Then I should go in the open. Good point.
DIONYSOS	Are you ready to go? I'll lead you.
PENTHEUS	Get me there quickly. Waiting is torture.
DIONYSOS	First, clothe your body in a fine linen dress.
PENTHEUS	A dress? Why are you disguising my sex?
DIONYSOS	To save your life. The maenads kill all men.
PENTHEUS	Splendid! Your cunning is right on target.
DIONYSOS	Dionysos himself put that thought in my head.
PENTHEUS	How does your strategy work out in practice?
DIONYSOS	I'll go inside with you and dress you up.
PENTHEUS	*Me,* in a woman's gown? That would embarrass me.
DIONYSOS	Then you're not keen to see maenads up close?
PENTHEUS	But I am! Tell me again how I must dress.

1090

1100

1110

[Handwritten margin notes:] now Pentheus' women

Pentheus would enjoy seeing the women on the mountain?

curiosity

DIONYSOS   I'll find you some elegant long hair.

PENTHEUS   And then? You're changing me—how far will this go?

DIONYSOS   I'll bind your hair and drop skirts to your feet.

PENTHEUS   Is that all? Anything else?

DIONYSOS   I'll give you   1120
            a green wand to hold and a fawn to wear.

PENTHEUS   That's what your *women* wear! Not me. I can't do it.

DIONYSOS   People will die if you battle the maenads.

PENTHEUS   That's right. Maybe we should reconnoiter first.

DIONYSOS   It makes more sense than to kill and be killed.

PENTHEUS   How shall I walk through Thebes without being seen?

DIONYSOS   I'll see that we travel through deserted streets.

PENTHEUS   That's a relief. The maenads *must not laugh at me.*
            I'm going indoors now to think things through.

DIONYSOS   I'm ready for whatever you decide.   1130

PENTHEUS   When I come out, I'll either be fighting, or I'll
            put myself in your hands.

            (*Pentheus goes into the palace.*)

DIONYSOS   Women, no need to aim our net—
            he plunges into it. He'll see the Bakkhai,
            but it will cost him his life.
            Dionysos, I leave the rest to you.   *ironic*
            You're near, I think. Take your revenge.
            First, destroy Pentheus' mind by flooding it   *psychological warfare*
            with perverse hallucination. Sane,
            he'd never wear a woman's dress;   1140
            delirious, he cannot resist wearing it.
            When I lead him through town I want the Thebans
            to laugh at his womanly shape—to repay us
            for all the ugly bullying we took from him.
            Now I'll go in to help him dress in the clothes
            he'll wear on his passage to Hades, sent there
            by his mother, whose own hands will butcher him.   ☆
            He shall then *know* Dionysos, the son of Zeus

*pure terror +
pure loving kindness*

☆

and the extremest of gods—pure terror
to humankind, and yet, pure loving kindness.   1150

(Dionysos follows into the palace.)

CHORUS   Will I ever again
arch my throat back
     with joy
         to dance
     barefoot
in the dark dew of heaven
the nightlong dance
              ever again
be the fawn bounding
     out—   1160
         into the sheer
green joy of a meadow

away from the hunters, away
from the beaters closing in,
     away
from the closing nets,
from the hounds
the huntsman shouts
racing toward my scent!

       Out there   1170
I'm the fawn rushing
like a gust
     of wind
into the marsh grass—
arriving, at last, among ferns
far back in the shadow of the forest,
where no men are.

What is wisdom?
         When the gods
crush our enemies, their heads cowed   1180
under the hard fist of our power,
that is glory!
       —and glory
always is the prize men crave.

The gods work slowly,
but you can trust them—
their power breaks all
mad arrogant men

who love foolishness
and pay no mind to the gods—   1190

but the gods are devious
and in no hurry—
                    they put
an impious man at his ease, then
hunt him down.
                    Therefore:
let no one
do or conceive
anything
the ancient law forbids.   1200

It costs little to believe,
        that, whatever divinity is,
it is power;
it costs little to believe
        those laws
which time seasons, strengthens
        and lets stand—
such laws are Nature herself
        coming to flower.

What is wisdom?   1210
            When the gods
crush our enemies, their heads cowed
under the hard fist of our power,
that is glory!
        —and glory
always is the prize men crave.

        The stormblown sailor
swept into harbor is blessed with luck,
so is the cornered man who fights free;
one man defeats another,
some in this venture, some in that.   1220
Men grow rich, or take power,
ten thousand men want ten thousand things,
most see their hopes
go to ruin, a few see them all
come true—but the man whose life
        right now, this day
brings joy to his heart—
is happy beyond harm.

*(Dionysos steps out from the palace, looks behind him
and calls to Pentheus, who hesitates inside.)*

DIONYSOS   Come on out!
Aren't you the man so eager to see
what he shouldn't? I mean you, Pentheus.
Don't hide indoors, let's have a look at you.
If you like evil so much, show us   1230

*(Pentheus emerges wearing a maenad's clothes—
long gown, false curls, a fawnskin and fennel wand.)*

how you dress for it.
                              Ah! As a woman, a maenad,
one of the Bakkhai! You won't find it hard
to infiltrate your mother's pack—
you could pass for any of Kadmos' daughters.

PENTHEUS   I think I'm seeing two suns   1240
on fire in heaven, and Thebes
doubles into two cities,
her seven gates are now fourteen—
and you trot like a bull, with horns
sprouting from your head!
Or were you always . . . animal?
There's no question you're a bull now.

DIONYSOS   What you see is the god—not hostile,
but helping us, since we've appeased him.
Your eyes now see what they must.   1250

PENTHEUS   Don't I have great presence when I move?
Tell me who I look like. My mother? Or my aunts?

DIONYSOS   I look at you, but I see all those women.
                                          Wait,
let's tuck back this curl. It's springing loose.

PENTHEUS   Inside I was dancing, throwing my head back
like a maenad, and it shook out.

DIONYSOS   Let it be
my job to make it behave. Hold still.

PENTHEUS   Please fix it. I want you to take care of me.   1260

DIONYSOS   Your belt's not snug. Look how your gown bunches
over your ankles.

PENTHEUS   It's bunched on the right,
but on my left side it falls perfectly.

DIONYSOS   When you see the Bakkhai, you'll find them
surprisingly good at what they do—
so good, you'll admit I'm your best friend.

PENTHEUS   How does
a maenad hold her wand? Right-handed? Or like this?

DIONYSOS   Shift it to your right hand. Now thrust in time   1270
with your right foot, and keep it high.
I'm glad you've dropped your old rigid ways.

PENTHEUS   Could I carry Cithaeron and the maenads on my shoulders?

DIONYSOS   You could. You can do anything you wish,
now that your sick mind has gone sane.

PENTHEUS   Will we need a crowbar? Or just my bare hands?
Shall I armlock the peak and wrench it loose?

DIONYSOS   Don't, you'll crush the nymphs' caves and hurt
the woodlands where Pan plays his pipes.

PENTHEUS   You're right. We must not use crude strength   1280
to overpower the women. I'll gain my end
by hiding in a fir tree.

DIONYSOS   We'll make this ambush
worthy of a skillful maenad-watcher like you.

PENTHEUS   I see maenads spring up and down
in their thickets like netted birds,
caught up in sex and loving it.

DIONYSOS   You have found your life's work: to witness
exactly that! You will catch them in the act—   1290
or it could be *your* face to which the blood will come.

PENTHEUS   Show me off through the heart of Thebes.
I want them all to see: I'm the man
who will brave anything.

DIONYSOS   Indeed you will.
The suffering of Thebes
is on your shoulders now. Yours alone.
Something violent lies ahead
and you won't miss it.
                              Come with me,   1300
I will see you through it.
Someone else will bring you home.

PENTHEUS   Mother!

DIONYSOS   Yes! As a great symbol to mankind

PENTHEUS   That's my wish.

DIONYSOS   you will be carried here

PENTHEUS   What luxury!

DIONYSOS   hugged in your mother's arms.

PENTHEUS   You'll make me go
            all to pieces!   1310

DIONYSOS   I'd have it no other way.

PENTHEUS   Then I'll have what I deserve!

DIONYSOS   You are amazing!—but no more amazing
            than the fate you go out to meet. Its glory
            will lift you like a god into heaven!
            Reach out and take him, mother Agave,
            and all you daughters of Kadmos.
            I lead this boy to his supreme ordeal
            which I—and the God Who Cries Out—will win.
            What happens next will explain itself.   1320

            (Exit Dionysos leading Pentheus toward Cithaeron.)

CHORUS   Chase him into the hills, you mad hounds
                    from Lyssa's pack!
                    Catch Kadmos' daughters
            in the fury of their dance
                    and train it
            on this boy in woman's clothes,
                    this crazed spy
                    hunting maenads.
            Agave, looking out from her high spike of rock,
            will catch sight of him first: 1330
                    "Maenads!" she'll say, "who is
            that Theban scout who comes up here
                    to spy on mountain dancers?
            Don't tell me his mother's a woman—
                    she's a lion—
                    or a Gorgon
            from the African desert."

            Vengeance! bring it out
                    into the open
            where every one of us may see: 1340

with your righteous sword
    cut this godhater's
        throat—
his pride is savage, unscrupulous,
he's Echion's son, snakeborn
      from the muck of the earth.

That rebel tries to shout down
    your mysteries, Bakkhos;
    your mother's cult
    drives him wild.   1350
At first he tries to outwit them
    but his boldness
    carries him away—
      he flails
at Invulnerable Power.
But death will soon set him straight.
The gods give no one
    a second chance.

Never question the gods,
    do what they ask.   1360
    Live quietly,
within mortal limits.
    Obedience,
alone, frees human life from pain.

    I don't envy
those who struggle to be wise—
though I might join that hunt
    my heart's not in it—it's in
hunting what I see
clearly—those great obvious things   1370
which make our lives graceful,
    worth living—
    day and night
to love the gods we hold in awe,
to defend every age-old truth,
    and forget all the rest.

Vengeance! bring it out
    into the open
where every one of us may see:
with your righteous sword   1380
    cut this godhater's
        throat—

his pride is savage, unscrupulous,
he's Echion's son, snakeborn
    from the muck of the earth.

    O God
Who Cries Out—show us *now*
what wild great
    beast you are!
    Be a   1390
BULL
    a
SNAKE WITH A HUNDRED HEADS!
    a
LION IN FLAMES!

Go out to your maenads
    where they're dancing
out of the maenad-hunter's grasp—
    ready at last
    to strike back.   1400
    Smile at him
when your noose wrenches his throat
    as he stumbles
under the murdering hands of
    your maenad pack.

(Enter Messenger from Cithaeron.)

MESSENGER   This house was once the luckiest in Greece.
Its tough old founder came here from Sidon,
seeded the earth with teeth from the great snake
and harvested fighting troops one summer.
But now this house and its people are finished.   1410

LEADER   What do you have—fresh news of the Bakkhai?

MESSENGER   Echion's boy Pentheus has been killed.

LEADER   O Bakkhos, what a god!
There's your power in plain sight!

MESSENGER   Do I hear you right, women?
Why this elation at my lord's murder?

LEADER   We love his death. We're Asians! Barbarians!
And now we have a barbarous song to sing—
now that your prison can't scare us.

MESSENGER   Thebes isn't so emasculated that it can't . . .   1420

LEADER   Can't what? Bakkhos tells us what to do.
                Not Thebes. Bakkhos!

MESSENGER   Look, I can ignore your barbaric speech—
                but why such pleasure when a man dies?

LEADER   Your master was an evil man.
                Tell us who killed him.

MESSENGER   That stranger—who promised to show Pentheus
                his mysteries—guided us out. I went with my master.
                We left behind the last valleys farmed by Thebans,
                we forded the swollen Asopus, then climbed the rocky   1430
                switchbacks well up the mountainside.
                We paused in a wooded hollow
                sensing we were near, mouths shut and moving quiet
                on the forest grass, to a safe lookout.
                No one saw us—but we could see—
                down a deep gorge with sheer cliff on both sides.
                Streams cut through it, and large firs kept it dark.
                There sat the maenads, working at pleasant chores—
                some stripped the withered ivy from their wands
                and spliced in fresh vines. Others frisking   1440
                here and there like colts whose painted bridles
                had just been lifted, sang
                Bakkhic hymns back and forth.
                Pentheus ached—that unlucky man—
                for a long unobstructed look at the women.
                "Stranger," he said, "from this spot I can't see
                those supposed maenads. If I were up
                that tall fir tree on the cliffs, I could look down
                on the lewd games of those wild females."
                The stranger replied with a miracle.   1450
                He reached into the sky and seized the fir
                by its crown, bending it gently, gently down
                full circle, until it touched earth.
                He made it perfect, like a powerfully
                drawn bow, or a wagonwheel rim
                cleanly bent from steamed wood.
                With ease the stranger curved
                the mountain fir into a circle—
                no mortal man could have done it.
                He set Pentheus astride a top limb   1460
                letting it rise, his hands braking
                the returning pull of the trunk, which straightened

to its full height without a creak,
the stranger careful not to throw Pentheus off,
as he rode high into the airy sky.
But Pentheus, even from that height,
couldn't see maenads. They saw him, though,
just risen into view—thereupon the stranger
disappeared and a voice sounded from the heavens—
it must have been Dionysos the god—   1470
commanding,
               "O my women, I have delivered to you
the man who mocks you, mocked me,
mocked our sacred lives! REVENGE!"
While he spoke a holy light
    flared upon us,
binding heaven and earth.
    The world hushed,
the air above, the whole forest
    stilled its leaves—   1480
no living sound broke the quiet.
Straining to revive that great voice
the maenads sprang alert, eyes flashed wide
searching the woods.
              God roared again,
the same horrible command. But now
the maenads heard him clearly, and obeyed.
They flew off like woodcocks
all over the watery glade,
clawing up the cliff face so high   1490
god must have blown mad power through them.
They looked up, saw my master, grabbed rocks
and stoned him cruelly, scrambling
from foothold to foothold
up and down the rock wall.
They slashed at him with spiny pine boughs
and shot their hard wands across the gap.
But the barrage fell short—
Pentheus clung too high beyond their frenzied
clawing, but he was treed, cut off.   1500
The maenads splintered an oak trunk,
fists cracking down like lightning,
and with the jagged staves dug at the roots,
hoping to fell the big fir—but they couldn't.
Agave yelled, "Maenads! surround that trunk!
Pull down that climbing beast! If we
let him escape, he'll tell all he knows

of our secret dances."
                              One hand
made of thousands tore the tree from the earth—   1510
screaming and moaning as he fell
Pentheus smashed into the hard black ground.
His life was over and he knew it.
His mother, like a priestess,
began to slaughter him. Pentheus ripped
his false hair away, to show his mother
who he was, to stop her from killing him.
He touched her crazed face: "STOP! Mother,
I am Pentheus, your son! Born to Echion!
Let me live!   1520
I've failed you—but don't kill me for that!"
Saliva poured from her mouth,
her eyes were empty, she was senseless,
totally possessed by Bakkhos.
And she denied her son. Grabbing his elbow
and digging her foot into his rib cage
she pulled until his shoulder parted, not
because her strength was brute,
but the god in her muscles
made the appalling work easy.   1530
Ino worked at the other side, ripping flesh away.
Autonoë and the whole pack of blood sisters
came screaming from their dance to swarm over him.
Pentheus threw all the breath he had left
into his own death-scream
which the women drowned out, yelping for joy.
They laid his ribs bare, their bloody hands
playing catch with his flesh
like children lost in their game.
His body's scattered over the mountain,   1540
parts strewn on the rocks, the rest in the forest.
We'll never find it all.
His mother is walking unconscious, she's spiked
her son's dumb-screaming head on her green wand.
She holds a mountain lion, she thinks,
and shows it off
down the ravines of Cithaeron—
her maenad friends are still celebrating.
She's yelling—coming right through
the gates into Thebes with her trophy,   1550
naming Bakkhos her partner in the hunt
and her partner in victory.

She's won nothing but tears.
I'll go before she comes,
I won't stay here, waiting for this horror.
The best wisdom is knowing what the gods want,
and then humbling yourself before them.
Mankind should hang on to that
if it needs something to live by.

(Exit Messenger.)

CHORUS   Now we will dance, now we can sing it out!   1560
Bakkhos wins, Pentheus dies!
That doomed spawn of the great snake
put on a woman's gown,
took the green wand of miracle,
the wand of joy which kills,
always kills, and went down
to Hades, led by a bull.

That wild roar from the maenads in triumph
turns over as it carries to us,
turning to suffering and tears for those women   1570
who fought their hard war, and have won
a son's lifeblood smeared on their hands.

LEADER   Here comes Agave running home.
Look at her eyes: she's mad. Expect
the whole maenad pack to arrive next
screaming their love for Bakkhos.

(Enter Agave, breathless, exhilarated. She carries the severed head of Pentheus on her thyrsos; later she will cradle it in her arms.)

AGAVE   Bakkhai from Asia—

LEADER   What do you want from us?

AGAVE   Do you see this ivy frond
I picked on the mountain,   1580
this blessed kill to adorn our palace?

LEADER   I see it. Now you're one of us,
a reveler. Welcome.

AGAVE   I took this yearling lion
without ropes. Look at him!

LEADER   You took him where?

AGAVE	Cithaeron . . .	
LEADER	Cithaeron?	
AGAVE	. . . slaughtered him.	
LEADER	Who struck him first?	1590
AGAVE	I did. He's mine.	
LEADER	Should we call you "Blessed" Agave?	
AGAVE	The maenads did.	
LEADER	Who helped you kill?	
AGAVE	It was Kadmos' . . .	
LEADER	Kadmos!	

AGAVE   Kadmos' daughters helped—
they were all in on the kill.
Our hunt was lucky, now let's feast! And share!

LEADER	Share *what* with you, woman?	1600

AGAVE   This bull! He's young. Blooming!
Feel his thick wavy mane.
It crowns him and blends
with the soft down under his jaw.

LEADER	He is a beast, to judge by that hair.	

AGAVE   That priest of Bakkhos
tracked him for us—O he was wise!—
then signaled our attack.

LEADER	Our leader knows how to hunt.	
AGAVE	Are you still praising me?	1610
LEADER	You can take it for that.	
AGAVE	Soon the people . . .	
LEADER	Start with Pentheus, your son . . .	

AGAVE   will praise
his mother, for killing this young lion.

LEADER	Stunning game!	
AGAVE	And killed in a stunning way.	
LEADER	Are you proud?	

AGAVE   Aching with pride.
        I have done something great for Thebes.   1620
        Killing this beast still makes me tremble.

LEADER Show us your prize, poor woman.
        Show Thebes what you have killed.

        (Agave lifts Pentheus' head high while she speaks.)

AGAVE   People of Thebes, citizens of our lovely towers,
        I want you to see this quarry which your women
        have just surprised and killed.
        No javelins you throw
        from a safe distance, no iron nets,
        only our delicate fingers, our white feminine arms
        did this. Men, all your clanging weapons   1630
        are for cowards. From now on, who will take pride
        if he lets steel do his killing?
        I caught this one, and my bare hands
        tore his limbs off.
                        Where's Father?
        He should see this. And my son!
        Someone go look for Pentheus. Tell him
        to raise a ladder to our palace roof
        so he may hang a trophy on the front beams—
        this lion's head I've just brought home.   1640

        *(Kadmos enters leading several servants who carry a heavy
        tarpaulin holding Pentheus' body.)*

KADMOS Bring him this way, men. Lay Pentheus'
        dead wretched weight down, by the palace.
        I found him piece by piece,
        I looked in a hundred places.
        His body was dismembered and hidden
        in rock clefts and thickets
        all over Cithaeron, no two pieces
        together.
                        We had just reached our walls,
        Tiresias and I, walking home   1650
        from those mountain dances of the Bakkhai.
        A man told me what my daughters had done—
        their hideous bravery.
        I climbed straight back up the mountain
        to find what I could of my grandson's body
        insanely butchered by those women, and bring it home.
        I saw Actaeon's mother Autonoë up there—

Ino beside her, both trotting deranged
and wretched through the oak forest.
                                   I'm told Agave   1660
came running here at a maenad's pace—
It's true. There she is.
I can see her misery with my own eyes.

AGAVE   Father, now you can boast that you've fathered
            the bravest daughters a man could!
            I say "daughters" but the daughter I mean is me.
            I quit my loom and found more serious work—
            now I hunt wild animals barehanded. Here's one
            still warm, cradled here in my arms.
            You must be fearless to kill this animal.   1670
            He's something to hang up over our doors.
            You hold him, Father. Don't you love him?
            Don't you want to call our clan together?
            We'll celebrate! You'll all share
            the glory of my success.

KADMOS   There is no way to comprehend this pain.
            What you have
                   in your deluded, murderer's hands
            is too much to look at. Yes,
            this is the noblest sacrifice   1680
            you could ever give this god! *This*
            is the feast you want to feed to your city!
            Pain crushes me.
            And will crush you.
            What the God Who Cries Out
            does to us is justice, barbaric justice.
            This god was our blood-kin, born
            in our house, yet, without one qualm
            he destroys us all.

AGAVE   Old age dries men up. They're bitter   1690
            all the time, spiteful and scolding.
            Let my *son* be a good hunter, let him
            inherit my genius for killing. Let it show
            when he hunts next time with the young Theban men.
            His only talent now is for fighting god.
            Discipline him, Father. That's your job.
                                   Call him here,
            let him see me
            in my glory!

KADMOS Hopeless   1700
      madness.
      When you find out what you have done
      you will suffer all the pain
      this life can hold.
      But if, somehow, you dream out your life
      in this insane euphoria
      you'll seem happy,
      you'll seem blessed!

      But you won't be.

AGAVE I won't? What could hurt me now?   1710

KADMOS   Stop!—
      look up at the sky.

AGAVE   I'm looking.
      Why must I do this?

KADMOS Is it the same sky? Or has the sky
      changed?

AGAVE   Much brighter now. *Much* clearer.

KADMOS Is something in you still soaring?

AGAVE Did you say *soaring*? No, I'm changing,
      I feel peaceful. My mind's clearing. 1720
      I'm not flying anymore.

KADMOS Now. Try hard to hear me.
      Can you answer a question?

AGAVE Ask it, Father.
      I have lost track of what we said.

KADMOS Who was the man you married? From what great clan?

AGAVE You married me to Echion. He was snakeborn.

KADMOS And the son born to you and Echion?
      Name him.

AGAVE   Pentheus.   1730
      We made love and Pentheus was born.

KADMOS Look down at what you're holding.
      Whose head is that?

AGAVE   A lion's head,
      my fellow killers said a lion.

KADMOS   Now look directly at its face.
Will it hurt you just to look?

AGAVE   Ohhh. What is this?
What *am* I holding?

KADMOS   Look harder.   1740
Force your whole mind to know
what it is.

AGAVE   All the grief there is,
I see it!

KADMOS   Does it still look like a lion?

AGAVE   No. It's Pentheus.
His head
in my hands.

KADMOS   My eyes were in tears
before yours saw the truth.   1750

AGAVE   Who killed him?
Why am *I* holding him?

KADMOS   TRUTH, you are savage . . .

AGAVE   Say it! Say it!
My heart's terrified. It knows.

KADMOS   And she's defenseless.
You killed your son. You
and your sisters.

AGAVE   Where? In this house? Where?

KADMOS   Out where his own hounds tore Actaeon apart.   1760

AGAVE   Why did Pentheus go to Cithaeron?

KADMOS   To sneer at you maenads. And at god.

AGAVE   What were we women doing there?

KADMOS   You were insane.
The fury of Bakkhos had crazed Thebes.

AGAVE   Dionysos destroys us, all.
I see that. Now.

KADMOS   You denied he was god, you blasphemed him.

AGAVE   Why was Pentheus punished for *my* crime?

KADMOS	Like you, he mocked and enraged the god.	1770

He's crushed us all—our whole
bloodline, with one murderous blow.
He hurts me worst, because I have no son.
I see this boy, born from your body,
you suffering woman, I see him killed
in the most heartless brutal way,
this boy who brightened us.
He was our future.

(He turns to address the corpse of Pentheus.)

My son, my daughter's child, it was you
who held us together. How this town   1780
shrank from your rage!
I am one old man nobody dared harm
because your warning glare protected me.
If they abused me, you'd punish them, justly,
and they knew it.
                Now I'm thrown out of my home,
stripped of my rights. I was Kadmos, the great man
who gave Thebes an army by growing one.
I sowed murderous seeds. And harvested power.
You I loved most, my son. And though you are gone   1790
I love you still, you blessed boy,
though you won't tug my beard ever again,
saying "Grandfather," hugging me,
"Who's making your life hard now?
Name that bully bothering you. I'll stop him."

All I have left of you is barren grief,
and you have nothing left.
I see your mother devastated,
I see her sisters weak from their tears.
Does your mind still resist the gods?   1800
Study how this man died. You will believe, all right.

CHORUS   Kadmos, I grieve for you. Your grandchild
suffered what he deserved. But the pain
you feel because of him is too harsh.

AGAVE   Father, where is my son's body?
Let me see it.

KADMOS   Over there.

AGAVE   Have his limbs been decently set together?

KADMOS   No.
Open the canvas   1810
Show her Pentheus. Her son.

AGAVE   What is this dead flesh I'm holding?
Don't say it's a man!

KADMOS   It's Pentheus.
I found him on the rocks, in broken shreds.

AGAVE   Father, you see my life
changed. There is no way back.
How can I mourn my son? Or hold him in my arms?
His blood pollutes my hands, my mind.
How may I in this wretchedness   1820
     touch him
in the pure reverent way?
I killed him. Now, how do *I*
honor and love him?

KADMOS   Mourn him child, compose his body.
No one here will stop you.

AGAVE   Father, help me find again his handsome shape.
From these horrible pieces
make him perfect!
I made him once in my womb.   1830
I make him now, again.
How can I do it—embrace his whole body
     and kiss him
as when he was a child?
Father, bring me his head.
Set it where it belongs.
I loved his face, his gentle chin.
I loved every part of him.
On his journey to Hades
now, we must leave him   1840
exactly as he was when he was king.

KADMOS   Child, that cannot be done. Look at him.

(She looks intently for some moments.)

AGAVE   With this veil I cover him
     forever
from all our eyes.

(Dionysos appears as the god he is,
on the roof of the palace.)

DIONYSOS I am the god Dionysos, son of Zeus,
the son of Semelê the Theban,
come back to Thebes, where I was born,
to make you face what madness blinds you to:
the power I hold as your god.   1850

Because he fought me, jailed me, denied me,
I unleashed appetites in Pentheus
only ecstatic death could end.
        To please me
he was murdered by those who loved him most.
What Pentheus suffered was justice—
he was blind to my nature
and to his own.

Hear, now, what you Thebans must endure.

Kadmos, I will change you to a serpent. 1860
Your wife, Harmonia, the daughter of a god,
I make a venomous female snake.
As snakes, you both shall drive an oxcart
commanding a vast barbarian army
whose killer hordes burn many cities.
The oracle of god proclaims it.

But the moment your army
crushes Apollo's shrine
at Delphi, you must disperse
in shame to your homelands.   1870

You, Kadmos, Ares will spare—
he will spirit you and Harmonia
to the Islands of the Blest.
These are not human words I speak
but words of Dionysos, son of god.
During all this crisis
if you had known what true sanity is,
you would have found
me, Dionysos, fighting
on your side forever.   1880
And you would be happy now, at peace.

KADMOS We beg your mercy, Dionysos. We admit guilt.

DIONYSOS   Too late.
When the time came, you did not know me.

KADMOS I know you now. *You are
Vengeance*—without feeling or limit.

DIONYSOS   Kadmos, you dishonored me. And I am god.

KADMOS   Gods should improve on blind human wrath.

DIONYSOS   We *do* improve on it. The agony   1890
            you now feel Zeus sharpened and shaped
            from the first in his cosmic mind.

AGAVE   Father, nothing can touch the gods.
            Or change their minds. We're banished.

DIONYSOS   If your Fate says, *Leave!* why
            do you stand there stunned?

KADMOS   Child, we have come to the final evil
            which breaks us all.
            I am sent to barbarians
            despised and old—a hated stranger.
            Over me hangs that oracle, telling me   1900
            I will lead a confused barbarian swarm
            against my homeland Greece.
            By then, we'll both be snakes,
            strangling our own holy shrines!
            My life will be an open wound,
            for I shall never die, never be blown
            down through the black peace of Acheron.

AGAVE   Father, in our exile
            we shall not meet.

KADMOS   Why hold me, child,   1910
            like a swan whose white wings
            shelter its useless father?

AGAVE   Because I don't know who
            can help me now, or where I should go,
            I hold on to you.

KADMOS   Nor can I tell you, child,
            where exile must take you.
            Your father is too weak to help.

AGAVE   My evil luck will go with me. Never
            will it let me come home   1920
            to you, my own loved country,
            or to you, house where I came
            as a bride: farewell.

KADMOS   Hide in the mountains, child.

AGAVE   I pity you, Father.

KADMOS   Mourn
            for each other, and for our dead.

AGAVE   Lord Dionysos dooms us in his terrible way.

DIONYSOS   *(From on high.)* And in what way did Thebes honor me?
            Disdain of fools was what you gave me.   1930

AGAVE   Father, farewell. Find safety and peace.

KADMOS   Daughter, I can barely breathe an answer—
            no one is safe.

AGAVE   Let me go out to my miserable sisters,
            my sisters in exile.
            Lead me away from Cithaeron.
            I hate to look at that mountain,
            I don't want it to see me!
            Let its rocks and its screaming dances
            bring grief to other Bakkhai.   1940

CHORUS   The gods can do anything.
            They can frustrate
            whatever seems certain,
            and make what no one wants
            all at once come true!
            Today, this god has shown it all.   1946

            (Exit.)

The Bakkhai was very likely one of the last plays Euripides composed. The playwright had left Athens in the spring of 408 B.C. to join the court of King Archelaus of Macedonia, where he died in the winter of 407–406 B.C. Several allusions to Macedonian places in *The Bakkhai* suggest that the play was intended to reflect and perhaps compliment his new surroundings and host. Macedonia also had a reputation as a place where Dionysian cults were vital and widespread. Euripides the Younger, who was either the playwright's nephew or son, staged *The Bakkhai* in the Theater of Dionysos at Athens, where it and two other plays, *Iphigenia at Aulis* and the lost *Alcmaeon at Corinth,* won Euripides a posthumous first prize which the Athenian judges had so often denied him in life.

LINE 3　*Lightning* To revenge herself on the girl Semelê (rhymes with Emily), with whom Zeus was conducting an affair, Hera, Zeus' consort, persuaded Semelê to ask Zeus to love her as he would Hera herself. Zeus agreed, and the next time he came to Semelê it was as a blast of lightning which killed her. From Semelê's body Zeus rescued his unborn son, Dionysos, whom he hid within a "male womb" in his own thigh until the new god was ripe for birth.

9　*Dirce and Ismenus* Rivers that flow through Thebes. The "e" in Dirce is pronounced. If I were entirely consistent I would have spelled it Dirkê, but occasionally, as with Kithairōn or Teiresias and a few others, I have preferred the Latinized form for the sake of euphony.

9–10　*godhead/you cannot see* In size and radiance a god's appearance would be distinctly more impressive than a human being's. Three times in his prologue Dionysos stresses his tactical disguise as a mortal.

20　*Kadmos* Founder of Thebes, father of Semelê, Agave, Ino, Autonoë and Actaeon.

22　*sacred* Kadmos' enclosure and consecration of the site recognizes Semelê's status as mother of a god. The Greeks also believed that ground where lightning had struck was sacred.

27　*Phrygia and Lydia* In most traditional sources the origins of Dionysian religion were ascribed to these regions in what is now western Turkey, an ascription which many modern scholars accept.

28–42　*Then I left . . . Thebes* Dionysos gives the itinerary (as Euripides' contemporaries believed) followed by his rapidly spreading rites, from their beginnings in Lydia to their introduction to mainland

Greece. On the antiquity of Dionysian religion, see Introduction, p. 3.

31 *Baktrian* Baktria included parts of modern Afghanistan, Pakistan and the U.S.S.R. Media and Persia lay between Baktria and Lydia.

33 *lucky* Lit., "prosperous." Arabia's spice gardens were famous in antiquity as the prime source of her wealth. Compare the Romans' *Arabia felix.*

42 *Asia* In this play Asia always refers to "Asia Minor," that part of modern Turkey that included Phrygia and Lydia.

43–44 *shrill/barbarian joy* A cry of triumph raised specifically by women to signal the victory of Dionysos.

45 *fawnskin* Putting on the fawnskin was a ritual act which submerged the rational individual beneath an animal identity with the Dionysiac.

46 *fennel wand* The fennel *thyrsos* was one of the symbolic objects always carried by Dionysos and his followers. It was generally taller than the worshipper, with clusters of leaves, usually ivy, inserted into its hollow tip. Artists later stylized them to look like pine cones. *Thyrsoi* also functioned as weapons, and thus illustrate the characteristic Bakkhic transformation of the peaceful to the violent.

49 *sisters* Agave's sisters Ino and Autonoë. Each was punished by grief caused by the death of a son. Ino killed her own son and fled, becoming a sea divinity. (Several generations later she will throw Odysseus a magical buoyant cloth in Book Five of the *Odyssey*.) Autonoë's son Actaeon was torn apart by his own hounds, a fate alluded to by Kadmos in ll. 460–63. See note on that passage. Agave herself will tear her son Pentheus apart in a state of madness induced by Dionysos.

62 *sacred gear* Fawnskin cloaks, ivy crowns and wool fillets.

74–75 *shock of my power/dawns* Dionysos may be predicting the appearance in his own fully revealed godhead at the end of the play.

80 *Pentheus* Pentheus was a grandson of Kadmos only in a symbolic sense. Pentheus' father Echion was one of the Sown Men, warriors who sprang from the earth when Kadmos sowed teeth of the war god Ares' giant snake. See Introduction, p. 8.

81 *fight gods* The verb *theomakhesthai,* "to be a godfighter," links Pentheus as one of the Sown Men with the Titans, Giants and other superhuman opponents of gods in primordial struggles. See previous note.

103   *Tmolus* A mountain in Lydia still held sacred to Dionysos in Euripides' time.

108   *Rhea* Mother of Zeus, wife/sister of Kronos, the Cretan incarnation of the Great Mother goddess. Her name means "Flowing One." Euripides equates her with the Phrygian Earth Mother.

110   *drums* Tambourines, a characteristic musical instrument of women's orgiastic cults.

120   *ecstasy* The Stranger's presence energizes his worshippers, both willing and unwilling. A Greek would know it to be a phenomenon which carries a person outside himself.

123   *God Who Cries Out* Lit., *Bromios.* The name means "the One Who Shouts," or "Thunderer."

125–27   *roared out . . . to Bakkhos* Lit., *Evohoe!* One of the cult calls whose function was to summon Dionysos. *Bakkhos* was also a cult cry, and it became an alternative name for Dionysos. The original meaning of both words is unknown.

132   *Come!* Here I side with Geoffrey Kirk, as opposed to Dodds, who interprets these lines as commands to the uninitiate to stay indoors.

147   *Kybele* Originally a Lydian and Phrygian manifestation of the Great Mother. Her dancing priests were the Korybantes, who appear later in the ode, l. 196. Euripides, in the fashion of his time, identified the Asian Mother with a Cretan double whose priests are called Kuretes, also referred to in this ode at l. 193. It is really the latter who use noisy rites—to conceal the cries of the newborn Zeus from his father Kronos, who ate his sons to prevent them from succeeding him.

152   *Find him!* The Greek literally urges the Bakkhai simply to "run," but what they actually do is "pursue" some manifestation or surrogate of their god. The bands of women, *thiasoi,* dance in the hills seeking Bakkhos, or his surrogate-priest.

162   *opens his own thigh* Lit., "secret childbearing recess." The Greek would indicate that the foetus is hidden in the male equivalent of a womb. Although "thigh" is the most literal translation here, "groin" would perhaps have the appropriate associations in English.

167   *bull-horned* The bull was one of several animals so closely associated with Dionysos that ecstatic worshippers actually saw him in animal form. Other animals so associated are the horse, snake and lion.

168   *crowned . . . serpents* Ancient vase paintings depict this practice, clearly common in Dionysian cults. Plutarch tells us that Olympia,

mother of Alexander, was addicted to Dionysian snake-handling. In Orphic myth Dionysos was engendered in Persephone by Zeus in the form of a snake.

173   *ivy*   Though in later times Dionysos was crowned with grapes, in the fifth century he was often worshipped with ivy worn by his devotees. Ivy is Dionysos' emblem in the first stasimon of *Oedipus at Colonus,* and it crowns the wine-drunken Alcibiades in Plato's *Symposium.*

175   *bryony* "Smilax." An evergreen creeper with clusters of white flowers. In Greek its name suggests exuberant blossoming. The closest English equivalent is bryony.

177   *oak and fir* Mountain trees associated with Dionysos in his role of mountain god.

178–79   *tuft . . . wool* Strips of wool had holy associations in many different cults. To judge from Dionysian vase paintings, as well as ll. 168–71 of this play, live snakes could be used instead of snake-like wool tufts.

182   *violence . . . wand* See note, l. 46.

187   *free . . . looms* One recurrent objection to Dionysian religion was that it caused women to forget their homekeeping roles as conceived by Greek men.

193   *Kuretes* See note, l. 147.

198–202   *drums, flute's . . . voice* Of all ecstatic musical instruments, the flute had the most direct connection with the god because Marsyas, a silene, follower of Dionysos, is said to have taught mankind to play it. Athene threw her flute away because she had to distort her face to play it. When Marsyas picked it up and mastered it, he was so delighted he challenged Apollo to a contest. Indignant, Apollo had Marsyas flayed, an act which later generations interpreted as the liberation of Dionysos from his corporeal envelope. Plato banned the flute from his rational state. The flute was quintessentially Dionysian because, unlike the lyre, it was capable of chromatic music and quick modulations.

208   *maenads* A general name for the female followers of Dionysos, meaning "raving ones." Strictly speaking, they should be his nurses and original followers from the East, as is the case with the Chorus. But the name was extended to include any woman who submerged her identity in Bakkhic frenzy by putting on fawnskins and taking up the *thyrsos.*

209   *satyrs* Most famous of the semibestial followers of Dionysos. These, like the silenes, were eventually imagined as goat-men, but in Euripides' time the bestial element of both satyrs and silenes was still the horse. Both are regularly depicted in sculptures and vase paintings as ithyphallic. The chief difference between the two races is one of age. The satyrs were young and lithe, silenes, old and pot-bellied. Both are companions of maenads, whom they often try to rape.

212–13   *orgies . . . year* The famous biennial Dionysian festivals—one was held on Mt. Parnassus—which were still practiced in Euripides' time and long after.

214–15   *mountain . . . maenad* The text here is maddeningly uncertain, but there is no doubt it is an extraordinary passage. The version I have chosen to translate suggests that the female follower reaches a climax in her swift-moving ecstasy that results in her own physical collapse, then in the melting of her own nature into joyous liquidity with the god; at that very moment (l. 229) the male leader of the pack is transformed into the god himself. The passage seems to describe the exact moment when the god Dionysos takes possession of his celebrant. To distinguish the god and celebrant grammatically, I have used the masculine for the god, the feminine for the worshipper. In the Greek text the masculine is used throughout, though it appears from the context that it is the female worshippers to whom Euripides refers.

219–20   *devours . . . goat* The Greek word here for "devouring of raw flesh" is *omophagia*. See Introduction, p. 2, for an explanation of *sparagmos* and *omophagia*. Eating the pulsing flesh of a slaughtered animal was an ancient and universal way of releasing the wild animal in the worshipper from civilized captivity. This act was at the heart of Dionysian cult practice. A tamer version is still practiced in the Christian communion service.

220–22   *hurled . . . Phrygia* A psychic catapulting of the worshipper back to the original birthplace of Dionysian religion, as a Christian might be transported to the Holy Land.

225–28   *milk . . . wine . . . nektar* Plutarch says, "The Greeks believed Dionysos the lord and master not only of wine, but of *all* liquid Nature." (*Isis et Osiris,* 35, 365a)

230   *Turned Bakkhos himself!* Another puzzling and remarkable passage. The Greek text says that "The Bakkhic One" lifts the flaming torch, which may imply that the god is suddenly incarnate in his worshipper priest. The question is similar to the debate about the transubstantiation of Christ.

231   *flaming pine* Torches could replace the *thyrsos,* especially at night.

248   *our mountain* Tmolus.

256   *Lotus flutes* Made not from the Nile water lily but from the nettle tree of the same name.

264   *Tiresias* Most famous of Greek seers, a Theban, and priest of Apollo. His presence in this play gains appropriateness from the fact that his blindness resulted directly from his knowledge of female sexuality. As a young man Tiresias had seen snakes copulating and when he struck them with his staff suddenly found his sex changed to that of a female. Later, by again striking copulating snakes, he regained manhood. He was blinded by Hera when he resolved a dispute between the goddess and Zeus by declaring that, based on his personal experience, a female's pleasure during the sexual act exceeds the male's by a ratio of nine to one. Zeus consoled him for losing his corporeal sight by giving him divine sight as a seer.

265   *Agenor* Phoenician king, whose capital was Sidon (in modern Lebanon). When his daughter Europa was carried away by Zeus incarnate as a bull, he dispatched his sons to search the world for her. It was while Europa's brother Kadmos was looking for her in "Europe" that he founded Thebes.

301   *I can't afford* I agree with Dodds in assigning this line to Kadmos, rather than to Tiresias, as the manuscripts have it.

327   *the sudden god* The appearance of a new divinity often provokes hostility in the orthodox, and always if the god preaches revolution.

345   *spellbinder, from Lydia* The Greek word for spellbinder, *epoidas,* suggests one who bewitches with his voice.

395   *future power* A prediction which came true. Dionysos was officially incorporated in Athens and came to share Delphi with Apollo.

410   *through Bakkhos* Although Dodds accepts them, I have omitted ll. 286–97. Several influential nineteenth-century editors judged this passage to be a later interpolation, and one can see why they hoped it was spurious: Tiresias' "explanation" is as bizarre and implausible as the original myth. The omitted lines also contain a lacuna and apparent textual corruption. Here follows an attempt to translate them:

> So you laugh at him because of the story he was sewn into Zeus' thigh? Let me explain the beauty of that to you. When Zeus snatched him out of the thunderbolt's blaze and took the god up to Olympos, Hera yearned to throw it out of

heaven. So Zeus countered her plot with one worthy of a god. Breaking off a piece of the ether which surrounds the world [he made an image of the child for Hera] to hold as a hostage [but, by giving the real baby to mountain goddesses, he spared] Dionysos from Hera's malice. Later on, mankind began repeating that he had been sewn into Zeus' thigh, concocting the whole story, and changing the word hostage (*homeros*) to thigh (*meros*) garbling the truth that the god Dionysos was once a hostage held by Hera.

The phrases in brackets are attempts to fill in gaps of sense in the text as received. The passage may be construed in several different ways.

408   *sprinkle drops* A great many divinities, including Zeus himself, were honored several times a day by Greeks in Euripides' time by pouring small amounts of wine onto the ground before the cup was drained.

416   *Ares* It was his snake which Kadmos killed in order to found Thebes. Ares is thus also a "parent" of Pentheus. By making Dionysos Ares' companion, Tiresias may mean that the forgetful exuberance soldiers achieve in battle is a genuinely Dionysian experience, though he identifies only the equally irrational reflex of panic.

423   *high ground between crags* The twin peaks of the mountain that looms over Delphi.

437   *chaste woman* Not a judgment universally accepted in Euripides' time. Although both Tiresias and later the Herdsman dispute Pentheus' accusation that Dionysos' rites are sexual orgies (apparently based on testimony of his informants), there is evidence that sexual license was an acknowledged part of Dionysian celebrations. In Euripides' *Ion,* for instance, Ion accepts as instantly plausible the idea that his parents, heretofore strangers, begot him while drunk and taking part in a Dionysian ritual.

446   *drug* Tiresias does not necessarily believe Pentheus has actually eaten a maddening drug. Dodds compares *Macbeth,* I. 3. 83, where Banquo asks without literally intending the question: "Have we eaten on the insane root that takes the reason prisoner?"

460   *Actaeon* Son of Autonoë, sister of Agave. Her punishment was to have her son Actaeon suffer a *sparagmos* like Agave's son. Actaeon, in the version Ovid tells, saw the goddess Artemis naked while he was hunting deer with his hounds. The goddess splashed him with water with which she was bathing, turning him into a deer. His hounds did not recognize their master and tore him to shreds.

468   *Don't touch me* Pentheus apparently fears the power (well known to many religions, as well as quasi-religious ceremonies) inherent in wearing some symbolic clothing or headgear that fills the wearer, even against his will, with the spirit of the cult.

497   *name means grief* Tiresias here plays on the relation of Pentheus' name to the Greek word *penthos* which means "grief," usually of a self-inflicted nature. Dionysos makes the same pun in l. 703, relying also on the Greek sensitivity to the fatality of names; e.g., Oedipus, "swellfoot."

502   *Lady Holiness* The goddess *Hosia*. Her name derives from a word meaning "Divine Law" or "Righteousness." Only here in Greek literature is she personified as a goddess, whose function is to inhibit all forms of blasphemy.

509   *Loud One* Bromios, "The Thunderer."

512   *Blessed* Dionysos' worshippers.

546   *Cyprus* Hesiod tells how Uranus was castrated in mid-orgasm by his son Kronos; the severed phallus fell into the sea and its divinely fertile semen became the lovely, naked goddess of sex, who was then washed ashore (usually depicted aboard a shell) on either Cythera or Cyprus; hence her names Kypris and the Kytherian.

553   *Paphos* Town on the southwest coast of Cyprus, considered to be one of the most holy sanctuaries of Aphrodite, where she was thought to have washed ashore.

556–57   *barbarian. . . mouths* Presumably the Nile, though Paphos is awkwardly situated to be fertilized by mud brought downstream by that river. The mud would have to cross a good deal of the Mediterranean to reach Paphos on Cyprus.

561   *Pieria* Springs on Mt. Olympos. Drinking from them gave one literary inspiration. Birthplace of the Muses in Macedonia. Inasmuch as Archelaus, King of Macedonia, had recently established dramatic festivals dedicated to Zeus and the Muses, for which *The Bakkhai* may have been originally destined, the reference may be a compliment to Euripides' host and the local divinities; but connections between Dionysos and the Muses of Pieria are also attested.

565   *Graces* The Graces had early cult associations with Dionysos; at Olympia they shared an altar.

567   *Desire Pothos*. Always depicted as a beardless boy, generally as a son or companion of Aphrodite, sometimes a winged "Love" pulling a chariot; but like Aphrodite, he is sometimes associated with Dionysos.

590–91   *what common men . . . believe* See Introduction, p. 4, on the connection between Athenian democracy and Dionysian religion.

623   *wrestling* Pentheus presumably infers this from the Stranger's long hair, which no wrestler would wear into the ring. Pentheus reveals himself to be stirred and troubled by the unisexual appearance of the Lydian.

632   *Sardis* The capital of Lydia's fabled King Croesus. Tmolus was a mountain in whose arms Sardis seemed nestled.

641–42   *dreaming . . . face to face* The implication—that if he saw the god while dreaming, the event is not to be taken seriously—is not one all Greeks would accept. Dreams could be deceitful, but were also one acknowledged means of communication between gods and mortals.

644   *ritual power* Lit., *orgia,* which usually means either "secret rites" or "worship." Later it came to mean "secret cult objects." It is not certain here which meaning is intended.

653   *wild dances of . . . god* Lit., *orgia,* which cannot have meant "organized licentious activity," as it suggests in English. See note l. 644.

——   *Pentheus supervises (stage directions, p. 35)* All stage directions are the translator's. The manuscripts include none. It is even possible therefore that Pentheus himself cuts the god's hair.

700–701   *You don't know . . . who you are* Perhaps a deliberate echo of Tiresias' taunt against Oedipus in Sophocles' play: "Your eyes can't see the evil to which you've come, / nor where you live, nor who is in your house." *Oedipus the King,* ll. 413–14 (trans. T. F. Gould)

735   *Dithyrambos* One of Dionysos' cult names, sometimes explained by the Greeks, incorrectly, as referring to a second door (i.e., a second birth) of the god. The dithyramb was a choral song to Dionysos which according to Archilochus was sung under the influence of wine. Surviving examples of dithyramb texts are surprisingly tame. Dithyramb contests at Athens declined in importance as tragic competition, which was also dedicated to Dionysos, increased in importance.

737   *male womb* See note, l. 162.

754–59   *There is evil . . . fight gods* This passage recalls the legendary history of Pentheus' family, the Kadmeians. Mother Earth, far from being kindly in Greek mythology, is the primeval enemy of the rational and law-giving Olympian gods. She engenders, without benefit of male partners, bestial beings such as the Giants, the Titans (who tore the infant Dionysos apart in his first incarnation according to Orphic myth), and Kybele (who originally had both male and female sexual members and so was the most fearful creature in the world); and she also bore Echion and the other Sown Men after she was impregnated by the dragon's teeth. The Greek text identifies Pentheus as a son of Earth, and implies that this origin is the source of his anti-Dionysian savagery. See Introduction, p. 8.

777   *Nysa* One of several mountains sacred to Dionysos. Nymphs of Nysa were his nurses after his birth from Zeus' thigh.

780   *Corycian highlands* Heights near Parnassus.

782   *Orpheus* Orpheus, like Pentheus and Dionysos (according to secret stories of the Orphic cult), was torn apart by maenads. The site of this *sparagmos* was often said to be Pieria.

788   *Pieria* See note, l. 561.

792–94   *Axios . . . Lydias* Macedonian rivers which the god would have to cross if he went to Pieria. Lydias flowed under the walls of Archelaus' capital.

——   *Earthquake (stage directions, p. 38)* See note on stage directions, p. 77. How were the earthquake and shaking palace represented to the original audience? Since the play was posthumously produced, Euripides would not have supervised, but he may well have conveyed instructions to Euripides the Younger, who staged the play in Athens. It seems reasonable that these effects were not literally but imaginatively and psychologically produced. Dionysos' transformation to a bull and Pentheus' hypnotic subservience to Dionysos are both mental events. On the other hand, from Aeschylus on, the Greek tragedians seem to have exulted in the challenge of technically difficult stage spectacles.

813   *Poseidon* Though in the time of Euripides, Poseidon is known primarily as god of the sea, it appears from the earlier Greek poets that he was first and foremost god of horses and through that fact, the god of earthquakes and oceans—phenomena felt to contain the wildness and swiftness and energy of horses. He is almost invariably a grim and dangerous god, though like Dionysos he combined a savage element with male sexuality, as, for instance, when he raped Demeter, assuming the form of a horse, "on a thrice-ploughed field." He was worshipped in Athens as Athena's rival and co-founder of the city.

858   *bull faced him* See note, l. 167. Another hallucinatory bull makes its appearance in *Hippolytos,* also as a symbolic manifestation of repressed sexuality.

884   *fight god* See notes, l. 81 and ll. 754–59.

905   *The god . . . grapes* I have omitted the following line which appears at l. 652 in Dodds' text: "Your words are a reproach to your god, a pretty reproach." But since this line has no logical role in the dialogue, one or more lines must have been lost. Rather than invent a connecting line I have chosen to omit the anomolous one.

906   *seal off the city* Pentheus' intent seems to be to prevent the god Dionysos, to whom he has just alluded, from leaving Thebes. But how does Pentheus know that the god is in the city? To do so he must accept the stranger's assertion that it was the wine god who freed him. Such ready acceptance of the divinity, however, runs counter to Pentheus' obtuse skepticism.

914   *Cithaeron* A high mountain visible from Thebes on which the infant Oedipus, an heir to the line of Kadmos, will be exposed by his father, King Laius.

994   *Iakkhos* Another cult name for Bakkhos, as the god summoned by this name in the mysteries of Demeter and Persephone at Eleusis just outside of Athens.

1023   *Asopus* The river separating Cithaeron and Thebes.

1025   *Hysia and Erythrae* Villages one would pass through while running from Cithaeron back to Thebes.

1030   *fire . . . hair* More imaginary flames, like those "burning" Pentheus' palace. Such flames were not an uncommon miracle in antiquity. In the *Aeneid* II. 681–86, Ascanius' hair flames painlessly as a sign that Aeneus should leave burning Troy.

1047   *King . . . welcome* Euripides' messengers customarily end such accounts of horror with an appropriately cautionary observation.

1050   *love goddess* Aphrodite.

1060   *Elektron Gates* The gates—Thebes had seven—which faced Cithaeron.

1097   *I would give . . . see that* See Introduction, p. 11, for a discussion of this sudden reversal.

1178   *What is wisdom?* ff. A concise and frank expression of the Dionysian credo, which celebrates the sweetness of violence.

1240   *two suns* Double vision is not an uncommon phenomenon in a visionary state. It can be exhilarating rather than unpleasant.

1244   *bull* In his mystic rites, Dionysos traditionally took the form of a bull.

1321–22   *mad hounds . . . Lyssa's pack* Lyssa is the goddess "Madness." In-sanity-causing Furies are sometimes represented as hounds.

1329   *high spike* The exact intent of the text is not clear. It could also mean that Pentheus is on the rock, which would be closer to the events shortly to be described by the messenger.

1336–37   *Gorgon . . . desert* The head of the snake-haired Medusa which dripped blood as Perseus flew with it over Lydia, thus engendering vipers in the sand.

1338   *Vengeance* Lit., *Dike,* which may also be translated as "Justice." Here the Chorus clearly calls on the goddess Dike in her role as retaliator. As they did when asking, "What is wisdom" (l. 1178), the Chorus invokes a philosophical concept followed by a barbaric instruction.

1391–95   *Bull, Snake, Lion* See note, l. 167.

——   *Messenger (stage directions, p. 54)* To judge by his language and tone, probably a palace servant or soldier, a responsible and sophisticated subordinate.

1410   *finished* I omit l. 1028 of the Greek text, "I am sad for you, slave though I am." It is very likely a later interpolation, borrowed from the *Medea* where it fits the context. Here it does not.

1413   *O Bakkhos!* ff. For the remainder of this scene the Chorus' speech adheres to dochmiac rhythm, one charged with high excitement.

1475   *holy light* Lit., "light of holy fire." The Greek might mean magical supernatural light or lightning. Such an increase of light regularly signals a divine presence. See Plutarch, *Moralia* 81 e on light in the Eleusinian Mysteries.

1478   *hushed* The silence of nature in the presence of a god became a theme for later poetry—an uncanny peace which precedes divine violence. Compare the eerie silence before the epiphany at the end of *Oedipus at Colonus,* a play written in the same year as *The Bakkhai.*

1506–7   *beast! . . . knows* Agave apparently does not see Pentheus literally or consistently as a beast, since she fears his reports of the maenads.

1522–24   *saliva . . . possessed* The symptoms of epilepsy, which the Greeks called "the divine disease" possibly because its effect was similar to a religious seizure.

1578   *What . . . from us* Even the Chorus is staggered by Agave's deed and appearance, despite their delight in Dionysos' victory.

1639   *front beams* It was a custom to hang newly killed game high on the hunter's house.

1712–46   *look up . . . it's Pentheus* This passage rendering Agave's return to sane consciousness describes a phenomenon known in antiquity as well as in modern times. Euripides seems to have been an acute observer of such phenomena and may have known that the process Kadmos follows was an effective cure. See also Euripides' *Heracles Furens* for the hero's return to sanity.

1805   *Father, where is* At this point there is a lacuna in the manuscripts. Starting with l. 1806, I have supplied a conjectural restoration. There is no agreement as to exactly where the lacuna should begin. We know from Apsines (third century A.D.) that Agave throws off her madness by recognizing various parts of her son and that she then laments each part as she picks it up. The lacuna was at least fifty lines long, but part of it may be reconstructed from the *Christus Patiens,* "The Suffering Christ," a twelfth-century passion play which contains a number of lines borrowed from Euripides, including some lines from the passage missing from this version. My reconstruction is based largely on these lines in the *Christus Patiens* and follows the suggestions of E. R. Dodds and others. The lines which cross the lacuna should be taken as conservative, in the sense that they do not include all that might have been said, and as bold, in that one must make many guesses in deciding which lines are from *The Bakkhai,* and in establishing the order which they follow.

1860   *I will change . . . serpent* Here the manuscripts resume. My reconstruction of the first three lines of Dionysos' speech is without manuscript documentation, direct or indirect; here I have adapted Dionysos' opening lines from the prologue.

1868   *Apollo's shrine* Lit., *Loxias,* the cult name of Apollo, from a word meaning "oblique, crooked, obscure, ambiguous." But here Dionysos gives Apollo credit for accurate prophecy. The Greeks seemed to have incorrectly associated his name with *lexis,* "speech." It was in any case by speaking obscurely that the god at Delphi was able to maintain his reputation for truth.

1873   *Islands of the Blest* In the *Odyssey* this is a fabled home for those who need not suffer the more common fate of mankind after death, selected not because of their virtuous lives, but because of their descent from Zeus. As elsewhere in Greek tragedy, a god appears undisguised and high above the mortal characters.

1888   *Gods should . . . human wrath* Euripides is the only ancient tragedian to share the Christian complaint that divinity ought not to manifest itself in anger. Elsewhere in Greek religion, wrath (*menis* or *orge*) is a regular sign of divinity. There is a similar complaint in Euripides *Hippolytos,* l. 1441. With the coming of Platonism and Christianity, Euripides wins and divinity is absolved of harboring unjust anger.

1907   *Acheron* Lit., "to the down-plunging Acheron," thought to be a surface river which descends to the underworld.

1924   *Hide in the mountains* The Greek text here is an unfinished sentence which reads, "Go to Aristeious." A line or lines explaining the reference is missing. Aristeious was Agave's brother-in-law, husband of Autonoë. We can only guess what Kadmos' advice to Agave means here; perhaps to go to him in exile where he had been since Actaeon's death. I have substituted the present line to avoid the puzzling irrelevancy of an unmated line in the manuscript, which disrupts the clear emotion of the final lines.

1940–46   *The gods ... shown it all.* This final exodus reappears, exactly as here, in several other plays: *Alcestis, Andromache,* and *Helen,* and with slight variations in the *Medea.* Similar and equally nonvital lines are given to the Chorus in almost all the other surviving plays by Sophocles and Euripides. Their authenticity is doubted by some, but they may have been necessary to signal the play's end or to help the Chorus off the dancing-ground. In any case they should not be mined for the real meaning of the play.

Library of Congress Cataloging in Publication Data
Euripides.
The Bakkhai.
Translation of Bacchae.
I. Bagg, Robert.   II. Title.
PA3975.B2B3   882'.01   77-90732
ISBN 0-87023-190-1
ISBN 0-87023-191-X pbk.